The Believers Manual of Biblical Understanding

Twelve Essential Articles Of Rightly Dividing the Word of Truth

The Believers Manual of Biblical Understanding

By **Chukwunulokwu Nsofor**

ISBN: 978-978-791-383-3

For further inquires,

Contact the author:

understandingthebiblelive@gmail.com

drcfyne@gmail.com

Editorial Services

Amen Media Ventures

Table of Contents

Table of Contents

First words

Do you want to read, understand, and preach or teach the Bible as God intended it? Do you want to understand what a text or book of the Bible meant to the original audience; and what the text or book means to you the reader today? If that is you, *The Believers Manual of Biblical Understanding: twelve essential articles of rightly dividing the word of truth* is written precisely with you in mind. Interpreting the Bible—discovering what the bible text means and knowing how to apply its message to our contemporary lives are the main concerns of this book.

There is a fancy word for interpretation—*hermeneutics*. Hermeneutics is the science and art of interpretation of texts, and biblical hermeneutics deals with interpretation of the Bible. (No quibbling about words, you may simply stick with, interpretation). It is science because it involves rules and tools, and art because it involves some application of skills and imagination. The purpose of biblical hermeneutics is to make clear the meaning of texts and enliven the word of God.

We see this in the ministry of Ezra with exiled Jews, after their return from Babylonian captivity. In the eighth chapter of the Old Testament book of Nehemiah the people had gathered and asked for the scroll of the Law of Moses that God had commanded. Ezra brought the scrolls and read it on a purpose-built podium, from early in the morning till noontime. In addition to Ezra's reading of the word, *"the Levites, helped the people to understand the Law, while the people remained in their places. They read from the book, from the Law of God, clearly, and they gave the sense, so that the people understood the reading"* (Nehemiah 8:7,8). And when in the New Testament, Christ interpreted the Scriptures to the two disciples on Emmaus road, opening their eyes, its effect on them was palpable. *"Did not our hearts burn within us while he talked to us on the road, while he opened to us the Scriptures?"* (Luke 24:31,32).

The basic assumption of this book is that a biblical text or book of the Bible has identifiable meaning independent of the reader; and that the reader's primary function is to first discover that meaning, and secondarily to apply or communicate its message to self or others. The handbook presents twelve articles or "rules" to aid the reading, understanding and application of the Bible. It is offered with the general reader and ministry practitioners in view. The topics are arranged in a logical (*chronological)* order; however, the articles may be usefully read as standalone or in a different order of the users choosing. Technical language has been eliminated as much as practicable, or explained, or committed to footnotes.

Article 1: The Bible Is The Word Of God; And Word Of Man

The First Article of Biblical Understanding states that: The Bible Is The Word Of God; And The Word Of Man - give attention to how one relates to the other

> *All Scripture is breathed out by God and profitable for teaching, for reproof, for correction, and for training in righteousness, that the man of God may be complete, equipped for every good work* (2 Timothy 3:16-17).

> *And we have the prophetic word more fully confirmed, to which you will do well to pay attention as to a lamp shining in a dark place, until the day dawns and the morning star rises in your hearts, knowing this first of all, that no prophecy of Scripture comes from someone's own interpretation. For no prophecy was ever produced by the will of man, but men spoke from God as they were carried along by the Holy Spirit,* (2 Peter 1:19-21).

Growing up a young lad in the breezy village serenity of unperturbed childhood, I had always presumed that God up in heaven wrote the Bible.

God would drop the Bible from up there above to whomsoever God wills. For reasons I still have not given a lot of thought to and remain inexplicable I would always wait with bated anticipation looking out from behind the scarcely fortified window of our house for Bibles to fall from the sky whenever it rained. *The brilliance of Bible and rain!* The heck that it never registered in my imaginative innocence that the Bibles would have come down thoroughly soaked, soggy and ruined in the rain water. Childhood days! I grew up to learn that God did not write the Bibles or drop them from above—rain or shine. Incredulous as it might seem, though, I grant seeing flashes of those infantile expectations during split moments of rainy unmindfullness. Miracles do happen, but all the Bibles I have owned or possessed so far have been either purchased from bookstores or gifted to me.

Christian theology speaks of biblical *authority* and *reliability* as well as *inspiration* and *inerrancy.* These are matters of fundamental importance to Christian faith and life, and we must frontend our discussions about biblical understanding with comments on them both. The Christian Church of all communions affirm the Bible to possess ultimate authority and hence the final arbiter of what shall be received and taught as Christian truth. This is particularly true of the *sola scriptura* churches of the Reformation (1500s AD).[1] (Some ancient

1 Article VI of the Church of England affirms: "Holy Scripture containeth all things necessary to salvation; so that whatsoever is not read therein, nor may be proved thereby, is not to be required of any man, that it should be believed as an article of the Faith, or be thought requisite or necessary to salvation" (Article 6 Of the Sufficiency of the Holy Scriptures for Salvation. The Thirty Nine Articles of Religion (Church of England), 1571 AD.). VI and X of Westminster Confession of Faith: VI. "The whole counsel of

communions—Roman and Greek—give a pride of place to the living tradition of the church alongside the Bible in that affirmation). Biblical authority, inspiration and reliability hold together. The

---

God concerning all things necessary for His own glory, man's salvation, faith, and life, is either expressly set down in Scripture, or by good and necessary consequence may be deduced from Scripture: unto which nothing at any time is to be added, whether by new revelations of the Spirit, or traditions of men.(m) Nevertheless we acknowledge the inward illumination of the Spirit of God to be necessary for the saving understanding of such things as are revealed in the Word...." X. "The supreme judge by which all controversies of religion are to be determined, and all decrees of councils, opinions of ancient writers, doctrines of men, and private spirits, are to be examined; and in whose sentence we are to rest; can be no other but the Holy Spirit speaking in the Scripture." (Westminster Confession of Faith, 1647 AD). Baptist Confession of Faith, Chapter 1 Of the Holy Scriptures "The Holy Scripture is the only sufficient, certain, and infallible rule of all saving knowledge, faith, and obedience, although the light of nature, and the works of creation and providence do so far manifest the goodness, wisdom, and power of God, as to leave men inexcusable; yet are they no sufficient to give that knowledge of God and his will which is necessary unto salvation. Therefore it pleased the Lord at sundry times and in divers manners to reveal himself, and to declare that his will unto his church; and afterward for the better preserving and propagating of the truth, and for the more sure establishment and comfort of the church against the corruption of the flesh, and the malice of Satan, and of the world, to commit the same wholly unto writing; which maketh the Holy Scriptures to be most necessary, those former ways of God's revealing his will unto his people being now ceased." (Baptist Rule of Faith, 1689 AD.

authority of the Bible is grounded on its being specially divinely-inspired (*inspiration*); and there is near unanimity among Christian communions that the Bible is without error (*inerrancy*), and therefore reliable and trustworthy (*reliability*). As with other historical creeds and confessions of faith, the Westminster Confession of Faith in the first chapter, "Of the Holy Scriptures," provides the full listing of the books of the Old and New Testaments, all "which are given by inspiration of God, to be the rule of faith and life."[2]

Note our two opening Scriptures above. In 2 Timothy 3:16 the apostle Paul writes that the Scripture[3]—is *theopneustos.* The Greek

[2] The Westminster Confession of Faith, 1647 AD

[3] The Scripture in this passage is strictly a reference to the Old Testament or parts of it. In this book, unless otherwise indicated or clarified by context, we shall use the Scriptures, Scripture, and the Bible interchangeably to mean the canonical Old and New

theopneustos—better translated as *out*-breathed rather than *in*-breathed—is the scriptural basis of our Christian doctrine of *Inspiration* of the Bible. Biblical inspiration teaches us that the Bible in its entirety is the written word of God. Thus, the authority and sufficiency of the Bible as the ultimate arbiter on matters of Christian faith and conduct hinge on the Bible being *"breathed out by God."* We should note that while the specific affirmation of the divine ownership and authorship of the Bible is recorded in the New Testament, the specific affirmation itself is indeed about the Old Testament. That is to say that it is indeed the Old Testament that is being affirmed here. The Old Testament prophets and other messengers of the oracle of God themselves were keenly aware of the divine nature

---

Testaments.

of the messages they brought and the words they spoke and wrote. Those words were not theirs, but were indeed declared as God's through phrases such as *"thus said the Lord," "the word of the Lord which came to..."* etc. By the time of Jesus and the early apostles, and in and through their words and examples, we understand that the divine ownership, authorship, and authority of the Scriptures have been firmly established. In due time, the divinely-inspired apostolic writings of the New Testament became recognized and affirmed as the written word of God. We use "affirmed" advisedly because canonization does not *make* a writing inspired Scripture, but only *recognizes* a writing as inspired.

Most Bible believing people will have little to no difficulty acknowledging and appreciating the divine authorship of the Bible. In most Christian communions and assemblies, the Bible as God's word is a well-established article of faith. For a significant generality of believers, the bigger hurdle lies with equally recognizing, affirming, and taking seriously the human authorship of the Bible. If 2 Tim. 3:16 teaches something about the *product* of Scripture, 2 Peter 1:20, 21 help illuminate our understanding about its *process*. We learn about the theandric agency and processes of biblical revelation and authorship. Free human instruments (prophets or "*holy men*") spoke (and/or wrote) as "*they were carried along*" by the Holy Spirit (1:21). The Holy Spirit was the proximate author of the Bible, man (holy men) was its immediate author.

The Bible came into being through symbiotic divine-human actions, analogous, we dare say, to the virgin woman's conception of the boy child that would be called the Son of God/Son of Man; which was accomplished through the action of the Holy Spirit and Mary being overshadowed by the power of the Most High (Luke 1:35). Or to a lesser degree, God's continuing creation of humankind. All of us, save Adam—are the work of God, and the work of man. I am created by God, and I am created by my parents. Thus, the Bible is at the same time the word of God, and word of man. The Holy Spirit elected and superintended the process of receiving and speaking and recording what God wanted said and written such that the resulting product can rightly be called the word of God. The human authors were carried along by the Spirit, but the process did not involve mechanical dictation, automatic writing, or suspension of the functioning of human minds. They functioned with their full faculties intact, fully grounded in their social, cultural, and lingual locations. The process did not have to obliterate or tamper with their personality, their linguistic and writing style, outlook, and socio-cultural conditioning—all of which came in handy in the discharge of their revelatory functions. The process is so specially divinely guided and guarded that the *product* of this special divine-human act *"all scripture"* is *"given by inspiration of God,"* i.e., the word of God—without error, trustworthy and authoritative in all matters about which it speaks. In a way of speaking, the Bible is very-God and very-human; not *either-or*, but *both-and.*

The fact that the Bible is not just the word of God or

Figure 1 Bible - word of God, word of man

the word of man, but at the same time the word of God *and* the word of man, is simple but profoundly crucial to biblical understanding. For therein lies the uniqueness of the Bible as like and unlike any other book, and key to approaching and interpreting the Bible. To lack this understanding, or to minimize the divine or human authorship of the Bible will lead inevitably to biblical misinterpretations and misunderstanding. As a starting point for biblical understanding, we must not only recognize and affirm the divine-human authorship of the Bible, but also the obvious and subtle ways one relates to the other.

The prologue to the Gospel according to Luke (1:1-4) provides a fascinating insight into the symbiosis of the divine-human actions in biblical revelations.

> *Inasmuch as many have undertaken to compile a narrative of the things that have been accomplished among us, just as those who from the beginning were eyewitnesses and ministers of the word have delivered them to us, it seemed good to me also, having followed all things closely for some time past, to write an orderly account for you, most excellent Theophilus, that you may have certainty concerning the things you have been taught.*

According to Luke in this prologue to which we will later return, we learn a few things:

a) The story of the person, life, and ministry of Jesus (the Christ-Event)—*things that have been accomplished among us*—was first passed around as oral tradition.

b) Luke was not himself an eyewitness; but, guided by the Holy Spirit, took time to review carefully and painstakingly:

   i. Eyewitness accounts and recollections.

   ii. Discourses (*kerygma*) of the "*ministers of the word,*" as well as,

   iii. Compilations of "*narrative*" by "*many.*"

c) Carried along by the Holy Spirit and drawing from his extensive research, Luke presented a clear, accurate and "*orderly account*" of the Christ-Event, i.e. the Gospel of Luke.

The key points to note here are, firstly, that the Gospel of Luke is a product of extensive Spirit-guided human research and writing. Secondly, the oral transmission and preservation of the story, and the entire process of Luke's research and writing were so specially guided by the Holy Spirit that the written final product—the Gospel according to Luke—is the word of God. The research and writing, though human in every sense, does not in any way negate the divine authorship of the gospel.

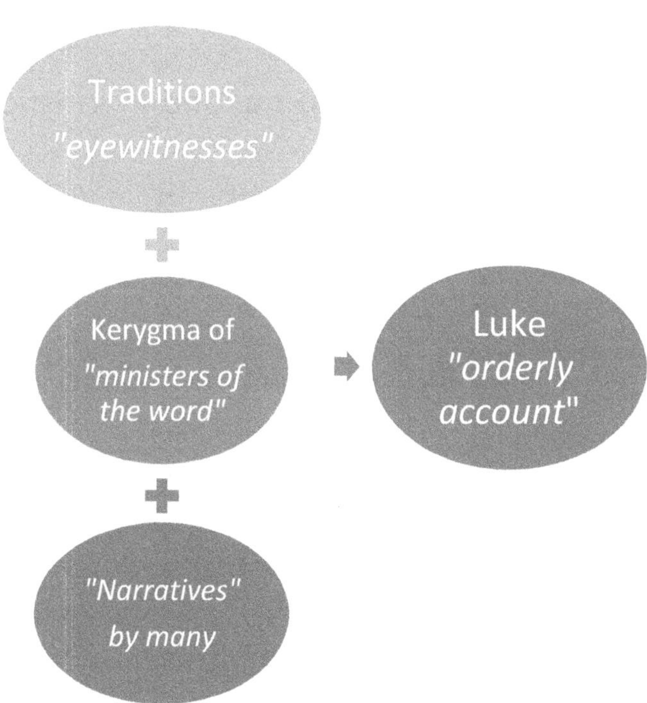

Figure 2 The Gospel of Luke - Prologue

Moses did not tell us in specific terms, and we shall be careful with establishing propositional truth from silence, but we should not be overly surprised if Moses would have drawn from oral traditions or other sources in writing the early parts of the Pentateuch.

To the extent we can point to the secondary role of the human authors of the Bible—employing human faculties, and context-specific cultural and linguistic tools of communication, we can say the Bible is like any other book. Yet, the Bible is unlike every other book because it is God's special unveiling of Himself in written form. It is not just that holy men put down the revelation of God in writing. It is that God initiated a special revelation of Himself, chose, enabled, and guided *"holy men,"* by the Holy Spirit, to put it down in writing as special revelation for all times and all peoples. The Bible is special because God is the ultimate author, and the entire process of Holy Spirit's inspiration and superintendence, and man's research and writing, are altogether the work of God.

As it is with the giving of divine revelation, so it is with its interpretation. *"The letter killeth…."* (2 Corinthians 3:6, KJV) is an oft quoted verse thrown out sometimes derisively to pooh-pooh proper biblical interpretation. However, such reflects the throwers' lack of attention to Paul's intent in writing a self-commendation letter that is 2nd Corinthians. God is the ultimate illuminator and interpreter of the Bible, accomplished by the same process of dynamic divine-human symbiotic actions. Again, the Bible is like every other book, and unlike every other book. The Bible is like every other book, because it is written by fully conscious, socially located, finite human persons. The human authors wrote with their full faculties intact. They lived in specific times and places within socio-political and religious-cultural circumstances.

The breath and limitations of their own individual knowledge or lack thereof were at full play in their writings. For the psalmists Asaph, "the Mighty One, God the LORD speaks and summons the earth "*from the rising of the sun to its setting*" (Psalm 50:1). The prophets Isaiah and Malachi and even the Revelator all wrote about the "*rising of the sun,*" all from their geocentric (i.e., from the standpoint of the earth) perspective of the universe. Today, we know what they could not know, that earth is not the center of the universe, and the sun does not actually "rise" or "fall."

Even if emphasis on the human authorship of the Bible is proper, one might ask, does it not reflect a low view of Scriptures or run the risk of diminishment of the high status of the Bible? Preservation of a high view of Scriptures is a fair and important concern for serious minded Bible believers. However, such objections overlook key points. To begin with divine-human authorship of the Bible is precisely a clear *it-is-what-it-is* teaching of the Bible and verifiable fact of history. Except for the tablets of the Ten Commandments (cf. Exodus 24:12; 34:1, 28), we know that God did not write or dictate verbatim the words of the Bible. We cannot do anything against the truth, but for the truth (cf. 2 Corinth 13:8). More importantly the objection may expose deep theological blind spots or profound misunderstanding about the nature of God and humanity, by wrongly conflating human finitude and sinfulness. It is God Himself who by deliberate choice—not arbitrarily, or haphazardly—incorporates humankind in the accomplishment of divinely-determined task this side of eternity.

The biblical witness paints an exalted view of humankind above any other creature as divine image-bearer. Of course, humankind is finite (limited) and not God, but finitude is not sinfulness. Not even the Fall with its attendant moral corruption could obliterate this essential or ontological nature of man as God's image-bearer.

While guarding not to uncritically endorse a flippant notion of intrinsic goodness of humanity, it is equally important to rid our thoughts of the opposite error of intrinsic badness of mankind. *Total depravity* is taught to affirm the biblical truth about the salvific barrenness of ungraced morality, that due to the Fall, human goodness or morality is incapable of achieving salvation except to the extend that humanity is aided by the prevenient grace of God. It is never taught to mean that mankind is utterly devoid of any morality or that the image of God in man is obliterated by the Fall, or that man is as bad as could possibly be. As devastating as the Fall with all its moral and noetic effects on mankind, SIN or sinfulness may describe, but does not define man.

Proper biblical anthropology holds humankind in polarity of majesty-humility tension, bruised but not crushed. Rather than see God's cooperation with, and incorporation of humankind in the accomplishment of divine tasks on earth as abasement of God, we shall see it as God's exalted view of the only creature made in the image of God. The Bible as the word man should not be seen in terms of a diminishment of the Bible's status. Rather, it should give us a glimpse as to God's exalted view of the human—the only creature made in God's image.

In the same vein, we get hints about God's view of human cultural and linguistic frames, artifacts, and customs. God seemingly affirming and utilizing human artifacts, cultural patterns and linguistic tools and symbols in communicating God's mind point to God's exalted view about those things. As importantly, utilization of shared human cultural and linguistic symbols and tools also makes interpretation possible and feasible. Imagine a scenario in which the Bible was communicated in a heavenly language with its unique grammatical and syntactic rules, utilizing imageries and thought patterns, objects, and contexts unknown to humanity. How would communication possibly happen in such a scenario? How would interpretation be possible, and right or wrong ones determined? We take such things as basic revelation of biblical communication, interpretation and community hermeneutics and doctrinal harmony for granted, because we have not contemplated a Bible that is completely and solely authored by God.

God in his infinite wisdom chose to author the Bible through human instruments. "Scripture has a double authorship…man…and God the Holy Spirit"[4]. In incorporating human instruments, God also adopted and utilized human conceptual, linguistic, and cultural communicative frames and structures. The Bible's writing followed the rules of language and written communication, including genre, character, plot, theme, convention, grammar, and syntax. As it is with authoring the Bible, biblical interpretation is not an *either-or*, but *both-and* endeavor. It is neither the work of the Holy Spirit alone nor the work of humanity unaided. Under

---

[4] J. I. Parker in "The Inspiration of the Bible." in The Origin of the Bible. Shared from PocketBible for Windows Store (http://www.laridian.com)

the superintendence of the Holy Spirit, biblical interpretation must take seriously the same rules of language and written commination. It is just as perilous to read (and/or attempt interpreting) the Bible as the book of man—led solely by human intellect—as it is to read (and/or attempt interpreting) the Bible as the book of God—led solely by the Holy Spirit. Each road will lead inevitably to misinterpretation, misunderstanding and error.

Article 2: Truth Is Constant, But Revelation Is Progressive

The Second Article of Biblical Understanding states that: Truth Is Constant, But Revelation Is Progressive - biblical truth develops and builds on previously revealed truth

> *When you read this, you can perceive my insight into the mystery of Christ, which was not made known to the sons of men in other generations as it has now been revealed to his holy apostles and prophets by the Spirit. This mystery is that the Gentiles are fellow heirs, members of the same body, and partakers of the promise in Christ Jesus through the gospel (Ephesians 3:4f.).*
>
> *For the law was given through Moses; grace and truth came through Jesus Christ* (John 1:17).
>
> *I still have many things to say to you, but you cannot bear them now. When the Spirit of truth comes, he will guide you into all the truth, for he will not speak on his own authority, but whatever he hears he will speak, and he will declare to you the things that are to come.* (John 16:12f.)

"Mommy, where do babies come from?" We are probably all quite familiar with this well-known

conversation between the inquisitive toddler and her flustered parents. Real or imagined, this awkward interrogation and the inquisitor's childlike persistence always seems to come out of the blues and often catches parents off-guard. How does a mom balance being completely truthful with her child with not overburdening a kid's mind with complex nuances which a child is simply not ready to grasp? Some back-and-forth till the mom blurts: "your dad puts the baby in my belly and I bring it out." Curiouser, our innocent inquisitor, with ever faintly burrowed brows, retorts: "how does daddy put the baby there?" On and on, till the mom or dad (who all along was within earshot and silently wishing, and pretending he was not aware of what was going on) figures out a way to distract the unrelenting interrogator and end the ordeal.

In his writings on the Scriptures, St. Augustine had proposed that the Bible is God's baby talk. This by no means suggests that Augustine had anything but a very high view of, and reverence for the Scripture as divinely inspired word of God. His contention though was that God's majesty far surpasses the Scripture, which was mediated by human subjects via human communication. Finite humans and human communication being inherently inferior to God's infinite mind, divine revelation of necessity entailed divine condescension. This also explains why a key principle of Augustine's biblical interpretation is maintenance of an attitude of deep humility and reverence towards Scripture. Augustine's schema follows from a deep realization of humankind's creaturely limitations while trying to grasp the illimitable, infinite goodness of God.

So, how then does an immensely omniscient God reveal the full contents of His infinite mind to finite mankind without overawing their puny time-space bound ability and readiness to comprehend and live out God's truth? It is to reveal truth increasingly, line after line and precepts upon precept, unto the fullness of time in what Bible scholars and theologians may refer to as *progressive revelation.*

We should be clear about what progressive revelation is and what it is not. To begin with, we make a critical differentiation between truth and its revelation. By its very nature, God's Truth remains as constant as God Himself. Truth does not change or alter with times, places, and circumstances. Unlike the Islamic Qur'an, the Bible does not teach any such doctrine of *"abrogation"* in which God changes his mind and replaces earlier truths with new ones. Truth adds nothing to, and subtracts nothing from itself. Not so the unveiling or revelation of truth. The revelation of truth is progressive. By progressive revelation we refer to God's condescension to the human condition and communication by revealing Himself and His will in the Scriptures over time with increasing lucidity. Each later writings gives more and more information and clarity than the former ones. This takes place within the Old Testament itself, and as the New Testament further clarifies and elucidates the Old. For instance, while the seed and prototypes of God's salvation plan is contained in the earliest pages of Genesis, God did not unfold His entire plan to humanity in the Book of Genesis or, for that matter, in the entire Old Testament.

Progressive revelation does not mean that the former writings are any less true than the latter ones. "Progressive revelation is not a movement from error to truth but from truth to truth, the lesser to the greater, the provisional to the permanent, the inadequate to the perfect."5 That is to say that revelation of truth grows and expands with time and circumstances of the recipients of truth. We begin the study of algebraic and geometric equations and statistical relations from arithmetic, not because the principles change but because the learners are yet insufficiently equipped mentally for those learnings. It is the same with compositions, legal drafts, books, and journal articles, which we begin by learning alphabets, words, and spellings.

---

[5] Alec Motyer. What Is Progressive Revelation 2018

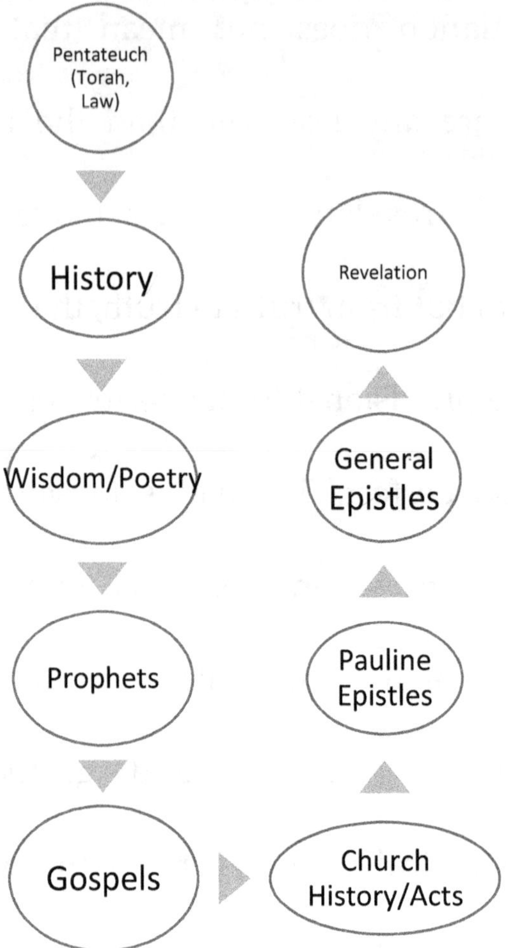

Figure 3 Progressive Revelation of Truth

In the English Bible's presentation, biblical revelation is structured to have progressed from the first five books of Moses, namely Torah (Law, Pentateuch), through the historical records (History), Poetic/Wisdom Literature, to the

Prophets, and unto the New Testament Gospels, Acts and Epistles. Behind this structure also lies an understanding of the progression of divine revelation. The Pentateuch establishes the origin of things including the covenant and covenant people, as proceeding from the inscrutable wisdom, sovereign power, and majesty of Elohim. History accounts for the covenant people's successes and/or failures living out the covenant. Poetry affirms and celebrates the covenant giver and covenant living. The Prophets call people back to the covenant and/or reprimand them for failures to live out the covenant, and pointing to a new covenant due to these failures. The Gospels announce the messenger and sealer of the new covenant. Acts & Epistles showcase the new generation of covenant keepers and life as new covenant people.

In the third verse of the third chapter of his letter to the Ephesians, Paul wrote about the mystery (Gk. *musterion*)—more specifically, *mystery of Christ* (v.4)—that was made known to him by revelation. In elaborating this mystery Paul provides us a New Testament way of understanding 'mystery:' not as something hidden, obscure, or esoteric; but as truth not well known to Old Testament people but now made known by revelation (v.5). The mystery or truth that has always been there from the beginning, Paul clarifies, being that God's salvific agenda in Christ has always been global in nature and scope (v.6). The truth of God's global redemptive purpose was already embedded in God's calling, choosing, and blessing of Abraham and his offspring for the purpose of being a blessing to "*all the families of the earth*" (Genesis 12:1f.). In fact, it goes all the way back to the mandate given to Adam, to populate the entire earth with bearers of the divine image "after his kind" (cf. Genesis 1:26f.). Indeed, throughout Old Testament history and into the New Testament, the choosing and blessings of Abraham and his offspring as God's chosen people were misunderstood in terms of narrowly adumbrated privilege. In fact, a good number of Jewish and non-Jewish biblical scholars and commentators view the book of Jonah as polemic against exilic and postexilic particularism and exclusivism.[6] The truth remains that rather than being chosen as a preferred special breed, God's choosing of Abraham and his offspring was for them to be ambassadors of His missional purpose of

---

[6] Cf. Stephen Derek Cook *"Who Knows?" Reading the Book of Jonah as a Satirical Challenge to Theodicy of the Exile."* PhD Thesis, University of Sydney, 2019.

reconciling and restoring the true objects of his redemptive love, the apple of his eyes—*all the families of the earth!*

God spoke (and wrote) through various mouthpieces ("*prophets*") across a multiplicity of spaces over time, but "*in these last days*" spoke definitively through the Son—Christ, who is "*the radiance of the glory of God and the exact imprint of his nature*" (cf. Heb. 1:1f.). In the *Hebrews* writer's reckoning, Moses—the high watermark of Pentateuchal and indeed Old Testament prophets and prophecy—pales before Christ, "*who is counted worthy of more glory, as the builder of a house has more honor than the house itself*" (cf. Heb. 3:1f,). As John tells us, "*the law was given through Moses; grace and truth came through Jesus Christ*" (John 1:17). The eternal truth of God's gracious lovingkindness embedded in Mosaic ordinances and statuses became progressively clarified and elaborated though the "the Prophets" and "the Psalms" (cf. Luke 24:44f.) and, leading ultimately towards the Modeler-Explainer-Clarifier-in-chief—even Jesus Christ (cf. Gal. 3:24f.). Progressively, legalistic notions of ritual sacrifice and performative morality continued shifting among God's people towards inner spirituality and personal morality, exemplified in Jesus' reformulations highlighted by such statements as *"you have heard it said…but I say to you…"* (cf. Matt. 5:21ff., Luke 6:27). A clearest expression of the idea of progressive revelation might well be in Christ's words in his farewell discourse of John 16. *"I still have many things to say to you, but you cannot bear them now. When the Spirit of truth comes, he will guide you into all the truth…* (vv. 12, 13). The Hebrew Bible (*Tanakh* – short-hand nomenclature derived from the three sections of the Hebrew Scriptures, *Torah* = "Law of Moses," *Nevi'm* = "Prophets," and *Ketuvim* "the Writings" (or "Psalms" (cf. Luke 24:44)) progressively bore eloquent testimony about the Person and Work of Christ the Messiah. Beyond the wildest dreams and aspirations of saints gone before, the disciples experience the physical coming, life, death, and resurrection of the promised messiah! Yet, neither them nor their followers will be able to receive the fullness of revelation or grasp the full meaning of the Christ event until when the Holy Spirit, the Spirit of Truth, "*comes*" and guides them (the body, the Church, see Article #3) into "*all the truth*" (cf. John 16:13). Through the Holy Spirit, we come to see in stark relief, and understand the truth of God's gracious essence and self-donating love in the voluntary suffering, death, and resurrection of Christ.

Led by the Spirit of Truth, the Church has been guided through the completion of New Testament canon, the exploration and explication of foundational creeds and doctrines funded and undergirded by biblical revelation. Truth remained constant, but full credal formulations and consensual orthodoxy developed progressively as the Church was able to grasp the *"mystery of godliness"* (1 Tim. 3:16).

Not a few may be tempted to readily go "aha, the Trinity" when they see "us" in passages such as Genesis 1:26, 3:32; 11:4; Isaiah 6:8. We will yet explore that critical place of context in biblical interpretation and understanding, but suffice to note that while the triune nature of God is eternally true and hints of which might be available in the Old Testament, a full revelation and formulation of the doctrine of trinity will await this later stage of the Church's readiness to bear it.

Hints of trinitarian theology may possibly be found as early as in the initial act of creation, where God (the Father) brought forth all things by His Word (the Son) and brought order and beauty out of chaos by His Spirit (the Holy Ghost, cf. Gen 1:1ff.). Yet, careful note must be taken of no biblical and contextual warrant to insist on reading back the later doctrine of Trinity into these passages. The text of Genesis 1:26, for instance, only tells us that

God (*Elohim)* was making the call to make man in *"our image."* The identity of the "us" to whom the call was made is not specified. The suffix *"im"* in the Hebrew language indicates (masculine) plural, such that Elohim is plural, literally "gods." The combination of plural Elohim and us in the passages often lead English readers to jump to the conclusion that God must have been addressing some form of a heavenly council. If God was not addressing an angelic host or the "sons of God," He must be addressing the Holy Trinity, so the thinking goes. But we must interrogate this interpretation as to its accuracy.

Here again, context is key, and both the textual and larger religious-cultural contexts of Ancient Near East ((ANE), of which the Jewish is part) will help our understanding of what might be going on here. Textually, we note that it is the same Elohim who "created" in verse 1 that is also creating man in verses 26, 27. While Elohim is plural, the Hebrew verb to create (*bara*) is in singular form, indicating an act of a singular being. We shall also note the uniquely radical monotheism of Jewish religiosity among the surrounding ANE polytheistic context. The Levant of biblical times was swarming with peoples, gods, and myths. It is within that ancient milieu of multiple gods and myths that the One Sovereign God will reveal Himself, and birth a new way of following that One God. At the very heart of Judaic religiosity is the *Shema*— derived from the first word of Deuteronomy 6:4 -- *"harken oh Israel, the LORD our God, the LORD is One."* In that surrounding ANE context the temptation to relapse into polytheism is an ever-present danger. While not implying inherent intellectual deficiency, it would have been as implausible of Moses to conceptualize and proclaim God in pluralistic terms as it would also have been highly improbable of the ancient audience to fully comprehend the highly sophisticated idea of the Trinity. One can point to abundance of hints in allusions to the triune nature of God in both testaments, but the development of a highly sophisticated doctrine of Trinity will take a gradual process over time. "This progressive revelation of the Triune God finally reaches its completion with the Spirit-inspired Ecumenical Councils, whose dogmatic affirmations elaborate, in perfect continuity, revelation contained in the Holy Scriptures." 7

---

[7] John Beck. *Progressive Revelation*, 2026.

The simple fact is that the ancient world of Moses' day and earlier had not developed the philosophical and theological apparatuses to even begin to conceptualize the idea of the Trinity. The people and circumstances were simply not ripe for the revelation of the Trinity. We must only rightfully understand the plurals "Elohim" and "us" not as plural of numbers but as plural of majesty. God's use of "us" in these passages are a self-refence speaking of His glory—His stupendous power to bring things to bear ex-nihilo, and authority to govern and receive due acknowledgment and worship!

Throughout its history, the Church has weathered through avoidable controversies occasioned by inattentiveness to the reality and ramifications of both the constancy of truth and progressiveness of its revelation. This often leads to legalism or demands of "slavish obedience" to laws, ordinances, and practices. Both Jesus himself and the early apostles battled pharisaic Judaizes over observances of ablutions and hand washing, circumcision, holy days, sabbath, etc. Till date, the same controversies—even if dressed in new garments—appear in such questions as to Saturday vs. Sunday day of worship, Christmas or no Christmas, and even potentially idolatrous what name to call God, as if God needs or has a "name" in a typical sense. Of course, God was known to Moses and the Hebrews as Elohim or YHWH, but God is also known to other peoples by other names. Moreover, insisting for all peoples at all times and all places in any name for God—which must be in a human language—either destroys the eternality of God (because human languages are temporal creations), or eternalizes a human language (a critical error of the Islamic doctrine of eternal qur'anic Arabic). We must understand the constancy of truth and its progressive revelation in Scriptures to be able to interpret and apply the Bible to our lives and ministries.

Article 3: The Scriptures Is Public Property

The Third Article of Biblical *Understanding states that: The Scriptures Is Public Property - submit to community hermeneutics—how the Church has interpreted and interprets Scriptures*

> *These are the words that Moses spoke to all Israel beyond the Jordan in the wilderness, in the Arabah opposite Suph, between Paran and Tophel, Laban, Hazeroth, and Dizahab.... In the fortieth year, on the first day of the eleventh month, Moses spoke to the people of Israel according to all that the LORD had given him in commandment to them,* (Deuteronomy 1:1,3).

> *And while staying with them he ordered them not to depart from Jerusalem, but to wait for the promise of the Father, which, he said, "you heard from me; for John baptized with water, but you will be baptized with the Holy Spirit not many days from now...." But you will receive power when the Holy Spirit has come upon you, and you will be my witnesses in Jerusalem and in all Judea and Samaria, and to the end of the earth."* (Acts 1:4,5,8).

One of the perversive Western cultural influences on Christianity is the twin phenomena of overly individualized faith and privatized morality. On one hand what is true and believed is adumbrated by individual whims and subjective affirmations; and on the other hand, right and wrong is largely determined by self-authenticating flashes of conscience. The tendency is everywhere present. It is present in the insistence on "accepting/receiving Christ as my personal Lord and Savior," "personal relationship with the Lord," "I am going to heaven, not we are going to heaven," "the vision God has given me," "my ministry," "my church," "my Bible," "what it (verse/text) means to me," etc. It is also manifest, in privatized morality in ranges of "we all know right from wrong" to "do what I/you feel is right," and "speaking your/my truth," and "do what makes you happy," etc. There is no question but that there are personal and private dimensions of morality and faith. Notwithstanding, we must be reminded that our taken-for-granted individualistic model of modern Christianity is more of adaptations of western cultural patterns than historic or biblical Christianity. We must recognize and resist the subtle but persistent draw to unwholesome individualization and privatization of faith. We must continue to return to a more biblical anthropological model of being human as enunciated and modeled in the complementarity of "male and female he created them" (cf. Gen. 1:27). That is, the human person as being-in-community. Of necessity, truth must be appropriated and applied to personal lives and circumstances, but the Bible and biblical interpretations cannot be reduced to exercise in privatized "what it means to me."

In the gracious providence of God, we live in a world where technological advancements in print and electronic media have made it possible that most humans on planet earth can possess personal copies of God's word—the Bible! The statistics are staggering. The Bible is the most printed and published book in history. It is, according to Guiness World Record, the best-selling book of all time, sold minimum of 5,000,000,000 units by 2021. "There are 273,972 Bibles sold every day, 11,415 an hour, 190 a minute, and 3 every second!" There is a Bible wherever one looks today, and in most languages of the world. This ubiquitousness of the Bible today often makes us oblivious of how extraordinarily farfetched even the thought of it would have felt to first century Christians—or just north of half a century ago, before the invention of printing technology the in 1400s AD. Prior to the invention of printing press, the process of reproducing such a large book as a complete Bible, coupled with the humongous amounts of materials, manhour and skills involved with the process, make complete Bibles extremely rare and very expensive. Today, it is estimated there are as much Bibles printed and distributed as there are human beings on the face of the earth. Which begs the question whether the proliferate availability of the Bible has been a curse or a blessing?

An assumption of this work is that we have learned and habituated sloppy and even nugatory ways of reading and interpreting the Bible, which can be remedied by relearning proper methods of interpreting and understanding the Bible. Coupled with the universal availability of the Bible and everyone with her/his own copies of the Bible, we are left with a petri-soup of competing autonomous truth claims. Subtle as it might present, we continue in the mistaken belief that our private possession of copies of Bibles translates ipso facto to private ownership of biblical truth. Hence, the Bible is interpreted according to the dictates of private fancies—fancies that may even be espoused as such and gloried in as "new revelation." Notwithstanding, it is a grave mistake that leads to multitudes of error. For *no Scripture (Truth) is given by (or for autonomous) private interpretation*! Biblical Truth is given to and received by or on behalf of the *ecclesia*—the called-out community of believers.

The two main iterations of the ecclesia in the Old and New Testaments, respectively, are Abraham and his offspring (called out for the purpose of being a blessing to all the families of the earth) and more narrowly circumscribed as the Mosaic "*congregation in the wilderness*" (cf. Acts 7:38). The second iteration of the ecclesia is the church of Christ or the Christian church, to which is given the *great commandment* (Matt. 22:37, 38; John 13:31) and the *great commission* (Matt. 28:16ff., cf. Mk. 16:15-18; Luke 24:46-49; John 20:21-23). Especially in the Old Testament, the covenantal pronouncements, stipulations, obligations, and ceremonials—fashioned after ANE Suzerain treaties[8]—required the assemblage of the entire congregation of Israel

---

[8] Cf. Meridith G. Cline, Treaty of the Great King, The Covenant Structure of Deuteronomy: Studies and Commentary, 1963.

to and for whom the covenant is made. To the assembled pilgrims out of Egypt—the wilderness congregation—the Sanai covenant was given. Some forty years after the Exodus, the second (giving of the) law aka Deuteronomy was addressed to the assembled second-generation survivors of the wilderness wanderings. (cf. Deut. 1:1ff.). These key components of the covenant include the second giving of the Ten Commandments (Duet 5), the *Shema*-- essential tenet of Judaic religiosity (Deut. 6), covenant blessings and curses (Deuteronomy 28) and sealing and preservation of covenant document (Deuteronomy 31). The Old Covenant together with its promises, blessings and ritual stipulations belong to the congregation. Priests, Levites, prophets, scribes and pharisees served only as custodians who functionalized and preserved the covenant on behalf of the people of God.

As with the Old Covenant so was with the New. In Acts chapter 1, reminiscent of Moses' giving of the second law, we witness the risen Lord's reenactment of the Commission and the promise of the Holy Spirit. Here Christ renews the promise and commission in the presence of the assembled congregation, for and with whom the covenant is being made. On previous occasions, Christ had given both the Great Commandment, echoing the fundamental principle of God's law, cf. Lev. 19:18), and the Great Commission, to the assembled body of believers. To them collectively he had given the beatitudes and principal teachings and principles of the New Covenant. The early apostles followed the

Lord's pattern and often addressed the epistles to the churches and congregations in specific locations (Romans 1:7; 1 Corinth. 1:2; Galatians 1:2; etc.). On occasions some of the epistles carried instructions for circulation among the churches in a particular area or province (Colossians 4:14). The Scriptures bear eloquent testimony that it is the community property of the entire body of Christ. We may each own copies of the Bible, but in no way is the biblical truth the private property of any individual believer or even a local congregation or denomination. By the same token, biblical interpretation or hermeneutics is a community project of the entire body of Christ. Community hermeneutics does not mean that the individual believer, an assembly, or denomination may not do the essential work of reading and interpreting the Bible. It means, however, that such work shall be done with careful attention to proper tools and methods of biblical interpretation. It means doing the work of biblical interpretation with an eye and ear on how the Holy Spirit has guided the church in interpreting the texts through time. Community hermeneutics means that whatever interpretive conclusions an individual believer (a local assembly or denomination) may come to is held as tentative and subjected to the scrutiny and affirmation of the body of Christ.

The foregoing remains true because the primary responsibility of the faithful biblical interpreter is to discover the meaning and message of the Scriptures. For the preacher or teacher, to secondarily convey that meaning and message to a contemporary audience. It is not of the biblical interpreter to add, subtract or otherwise distort or detract from the meaning and message of the Bible. It is not to propound and propagate peculiar, novel, fanciful and/or so-called "deep spiritual" meanings or "rhema," so called. As a servant of God and his church, it is to painstakingly employ the right kind of interpretive tools, and in concert with the body, discover the meaning and message of the Bible—that which only must be believed and taught as public truth. It is a task to be done with careful attention to how the body has interpreted the text or Scriptures throughout history. It involves understanding and applying proper methods and rules of biblical interpretation. It involves comparing one's methods and tentative conclusions with the methods and conclusions of fellow believers—ancient and modern. Furthermore, it involves submitting and subjecting one's methods and tentative conclusions to the scrutiny of fellow biblical interpreters. This is an awesome responsibility which as a steward of divine truth must be approached with holy fear and trembling.

Article 4: The Bible is Simple in Complexity, and Complex in Simplicity

The Fourth Article of Biblical Understanding states that: The Bible is Simple in Complexity, and Complex in Simplicity – work the complex to arrive at the simple

> *And he said to them, "Therefore every scribe who has been trained for the kingdom of heaven is like a master of a house, who brings out of his treasure what is new and what is old."* (Matthew 13:52).

Remember the book *"All I Really Need to Know I Learned in Sunday School?"*[9] Some adaptations of it might say: "all I need to go the heaven I learned in Sunday school" or "all I need to understand the Bible I learnt (will learn) from the Holy Spirit." When I was a little boy growing up in my village, I used to hear a common saying which loosely translates in effect that "the Bible is like a

---

[9] Cliff Schimmels, 1969

(labyrinthian) thick forest." Especially in the older mainline denominations of those days the parishioner was often warned of the extreme denseness of the Bible. Expressed or implied in the unfortunate warning is the notion that the Bible is of such complexity that one had better stay out from wading into it. Thank God, of course, that we do not need a PhD in Bible, Hermeneutics, Hebrew, Greek or any of the cognate disciplines to read and gain some understanding of the Bible. Nor do we necessarily need seminary education or degrees of any sort to be able to exhort one another in righteousness and welldoing. We do not all have to be Bible scholars, bless our hearts!

We are, however, not to be lulled into complacency by the apparent simplicity of the Bible. Jesus' timeless words in Matthew 13:52 (quoted above) hints to the complexity of the word of God, and as well teach us something about the indispensability of extensive training and skillful handling of the Scriptures. Not only the Lord here, but also in the quintessential Old Testament scribe, Ezra (cf. Ezra 7:6), do we see the type of training, rigor and skill demanded by the scribal tradition. Ezra's journey to wholesome stewardship of God's word led through dedication to inquiry, practice, and teaching (or otherwise, orthodoxy (or right belief), orthopraxis (or right modelling) and pedagogy (effective communication of truth (cf. Ezra 7:10)).

Jesus is often acknowledged as the Great Teacher. In Matthew chapter 14, the Lord had employed seven parables to unlock the *mysteries of the kingdom*

(Matt. 13:11 KJV); and provide resolution to an enigmatic dilemma about Daniel's vision of the coming *kingdom of God.* Daniel had seen and proclaimed a good news vision of a future reign of righteousness. The twin foci of Daniel's vision of what was to be the messianic rule were that it will a), overwhelm and conquer all earthly powers, and b), purge all sin and evil from the earth (Daniel 2:13-14, 44; 7:14, 27). This was the good news (gospel) of the kingdom preached among the Jews for more than 400 years of messianic expectation. Fast forward, and now here came John (the Baptist) and Jesus announcing that the expected kingdom had indeed come (cf. Mark 1:14; Matthew 4:17)! Which begged the question: if the kingdom had indeed come, and Jesus was the expected messiah; how come the Romans were still in charge and sin abounded? These perplexing questions the Master of the scribal house will painstakingly elucidate through the narrative analogies of the seven parables. Together they explain the nature of man and reality of moral agency, the process, the product, the cost, and goal of the kingdom. Yes, the kingdom *has come* in the first coming of the Lord; but the kingdom has *not yet* come in its fullness, and continues in its unfolding till the second coming of the Lord. Through painstaking inquiry and skillful exercise, the trained scribe made the complex question of the *gospel of the kingdom of God* simple. Complexity is simplified by skillful exercise of creative imagination.

The Bible was written, copied, and translated in ancient and modern human languages. With relative facility in any or more of the languages of the Bible coupled with commensurate effort and care, anyone could gain appreciable and usable understanding of the Bible. Yet again, we should never let the accessibility and apparent simplicity of the Bible fool us. It takes significant amount of training, skill, and rigor to be able to *bring out* of the treasure house that is the word of God *what is new and what is old* (cf. Matthew 13:52). It is not in vain that a couple thousand years ago the Apostle James (cf. James 3:1), in concord with ancient Jewish sages, had warned his audience about the awesome responsibility and potential danger in aspiring to teach truth. Those who aspire to teach must be wary of the severity of judgement from teaching error and leading others astray. It is that serious! We all must do well to heed those warnings even much more today, especially in the light of a highly democratized, diffused, denominationalized, and *I-too-can-cast* Christo-religious landscape.

Why is the Bible such a very complex piece of literature? For starters, though now bounded as one book, the Bible is indeed a collection of a tens of books. Each book of the Bible—Revelation, Romans, Mark, Amos, Isaiah, Kings all the way down to Genesis—is a complete stand-alone work. The books were written or compiled by diverse array of human authors, who come from an admixture of socio-cultural locations and linguistic backgrounds—Hebrew, Akkadian, Ugaritic, Aramaic, and Greek. These books were written or compiled over an extended period—no less than a thousand years! To that we add the problem of distanciation—i.e., the cultural gap between biblical times and our present time. That is to say, the several thousands of years—and the progress of human culture, knowledge, and technology—between the original characters, authors, audience of the Bible and us, the reader today.

The readers today do not only live in worlds wide apart from the original authors in terms of time, geography, and ethno-linguistic people groupings. The reader is also distanced by ever-changing family, social and ethical structures. Furthermore, diachronic variations within living languages pose additional challenges. English readers of the Bible may be struck or confused by the apparent 'meaninglessness,' 'confusion,' or 'contradiction' of some verse or verses of the Bible. *Apparent* because they may only appear, but not necessarily, so on casual observation. Take the simple word "prevent," and note it in these KJV verses (emphases added):

> *The God of my mercy shall* ***prevent*** *me: God shall let me see my desire upon mine enemies.* Psalms 59:10 (KJV)
>
> *O remember not against us former iniquities: let thy tender mercies speedily* ***prevent*** *us: for we are brought very low.* Psalms 79:8 (KJV)
>
> *But unto thee have I cried, O LORD; and in the morning shall my prayer* ***prevent*** *thee.* Psalms 88:13 (KJV)
>
> *For this we say unto you by the word of the Lord, that we which are alive and remain unto the coming of the Lord shall not* ***prevent*** *them which are asleep.* 1 Thessalonians 4:15 (KJV)

Reading these verses today, we may scratch our heads as to how and why the psalmist may entreat the God of mercy to 'hinder' him (59:10), or intercede that God's tender mercies shall speedily 'hinder' them (79:8), or that his morning prayer shall 'hinder' God (88:13). In the same vein, we may be confused about the apparent no brainer of the Apostle Paul reminding the Thessalonian believers that at Christ's coming, they who might be alive, would not hinder those who had died in the Lord. *Duh!* The resolution is, however, simpler than it first appears. It lies in the distance of time, and variations within English language in just over the last couple hundred years or so. The English Bible reader in the 17th and 18th centuries would have had no problems whatsoever reading and understanding these passages. Why so? Glad you asked. Notice that all the passages in question are taken from the King James Version (KJV)—a translation of the Bible.

The KJV was a rendition of the original Scriptures in the English of the 17th century Jacobean era. Over the passage of time, words of a living language, their meanings and usage change, and the changes affect the meanings of original Scriptures translated into it. The "King James Only"[10] or KJV heavily-dependent Bible reader today is at a distinct disadvantage and at real risk of misreading and misinterpreting the Bible. For the historical generation of the so-called Nigeria Civil-War Revival of late 1960s-early 1970s in Nigeria as elsewhere, the KJV was "the Bible," just as *Dake's*[11] and *Thompson*[12] and to some degree, Scoffield[13],

---

[10] Cf. Benjamin G. Wilkinson, 1930. *Our Authorized Bible Vindicated*; Fuller Davis Otis, *Which Bible?* Trinitarian Bible Society; 2015 *Manual* of the Bible Missionary Church; 2021 Dunkard Brethren Church.

[11] *Dake Annotated Reference Bible* KJV

[12] KJV, *Thompson Chain-Reference Bible*

[13] *The Scoffield Study Bible* KJV

Berkhof[14] and/or Hagin Faith Library pamphlets[15] were the seminaries.

The apparent confusion we encounter in the passages above lies only in the mind of the modern reader of the KJV due to changes within English language between the Jacobean and modern English eras. Etymologically, the English word 'prevent' came from the Latin words *prae* = before and *venire* = come, i.e., prevent = come before. This was the ordinary meaning of the word, and it was the sense in which the translators of King James version of the Bible used it. Over time the English word 'prevent' has metamorphosed in its meaning to today's common usage, in which 'prevent' = hinder. Modern translations, such as New

---

[14] Louis Berkhof, *Systematic Theology*

[15] Kenneth Hagin Faith Library Publications.

International Version (NIV), English Standard Version (ESV), New American Standard Bible (NASB), & New King James Version (NKJV), rightly translate the original Hebrew of Psalm 88:13 as "comes before." It is not that the modern translations are "omitting," "corrupting," or "changing" the word of God. It is rather that obsolete KJV English is now clouding and altering the meaning of God's word due to changes in the English language. And due to those changes in the English language, today's readers of King James would very easily make costly but avoidable interpretative errors of the written word of God. A starting point is to read—especially difficult or obscure—texts and/or even the Scriptures in multiple translations of the Bible.

A version or translation of the Bible is a rendition or reproduction of (the same) original Scriptures into a living language of a people. A translation or version is not a new or different Bible (as erroneously assumed by some less informed critics of the Bible). It is not an effort to rewrite the Bible or alter its original meaning. The need for a new translation of the Bible may arise because of a) discoveries of new or variant manuscripts, b) advances of research and scholarship in biblical interpretation and translation, and c) dynamism of human cultures and changes in living languages. Any translation of the Bible—no matter how accurate and trustworthy in the time being—will inevitably become increasingly obsolete, cloud the word of God, and eventually fossilize due simply to the passage of time.

Translation questions and variations between and within original and living languages of the Bible is just a sliver of the myriads of issues which influence and impact meaning and message of the Bible. There are also geographic, cultural, and other contextual issues. All these factors and more add to that complexity, and implicate upon the meaning and message of the text. As we will explore further especially in Article #9, there is significant difference between the related activities of interpretation and application—'what does it mean?' and 'what does it mean for me/us? In reading and studying the Scriptures for personal growth and enrichment or for public teaching and admonition, care must be taken to separate between interpretation and application. It is a very costly mistake which leads inevitably to misinterpretation and misunderstanding of the Bible to rush into applying the Bible or verses, texts, or portions of it, without first and foremost working hard to determine meaning and message of texts or Scriptures.

Discovering the meaning and message of a text, book of the Bible or the entire Bible itself, involves serious heavy lifting interpretative work. Faithfull stewardship of the word of God demands it; and yes, requires a degree of sophistication and skill to draw out the meaning of text and simplify its implications (message) for readers today. It is practically impossible to simplify the message of the Bible without first doing the difficult but highly rewarding work of resolving its complexity.

Article 5: Chapter And Verse Divisions Are Helpful Tools That Hinder Biblical Understanding

The Fifth Article of Biblical Understanding states that: Chapter And Verse Divisions Are Helpful Tools That Hinder Biblical Understanding - always remember God did not reveal Scriptures in chapters and verses

> *And the LORD said to Moses, "Make a fiery serpent and set it on a pole, and everyone who is bitten, when he sees it, shall live." So Moses made a bronze serpent and set it on a pole. And if a serpent bit anyone, he would look at the bronze serpent and live (Numbers 21:8-9).*

> *He removed the high places and broke the pillars and cut down the Asherah. And he broke in pieces the bronze serpent that Moses had made, for until those days the people of Israel had made offerings to it ((it was called Nehushtan. 2 Kings 18:4).*

There seems to be this phenomenon in human affairs that whatever could go wrong, inevitably does. Simple guide to right relationships eventually become legalistic burdens too heavy to carry.

Worthy attentiveness to the covenant principles calcifies into layers upon layers of pharisaic 'building a hedge around the law.' Humans become made for sabbath instead of the other way round. Moments congeal into movements, and ultimately fossilize into monuments. It is the way of mankind.

It was some thirty-eight years since the exodus and into their wilderness wandering, and the Israelites have been enabled to score a victory over the Canaanites at Hormah (cf. Numbers 21:3f). Scarcely had they set out from Mt Hor towards Edom before resorting to the ever-present complaining and murmuring, and badmouthing both God and Moses. *"Why have you brought us up out of Egypt to die in the wilderness? For there is no food and no water, and we loathe this worthless food,"*

(Numbers 21:5). Therefore, the Lord "sent" venomous snakes which had caused numerous deaths among the recalcitrant multitude. The people quickly came to their senses and in repentance pleaded with Moses to entreat the Lord on their behalf. On God's specific instruction, Moses made a bronze (most likely, copper) snake and raised it on a pole so that snake-bite victims who looked upon it could be healed and not die of it. With the passage of time, of Moses, and the original characters, these ordinary relics of long-gone era were gathered, preserved, and ultimately venerated as objects of worship. A snare to God's people which took the youthful reforms of King Hezekiah—some 750 years later(!)—to be totally smashed and eradicated from the temple (2 Kings

18:4; cf. 2 Chronicles 29:29ff.). Such is how the road to perdition is often paved by good intentions.

Chapter and verse divisions in the Bible might as well be our modern-day *bronze serpent*! We have become so familiar with seeing the Bible divided in chapters and verses that it is almost impossible for us to imagine the Bible without them. It might come as a surprise to many being made aware that neither Jesus nor the early church read the Bible in chapters and verses. The truth however, is that God did not reveal the Bible in chapters and verses. Neither did the biblical writers write the Bible in chapters and verses. Chapter and verse divisions was a manmade tool to aid reading and comprehension of Scriptures. However, what was well meant as an aid to biblical understanding might have turned into our Achilles heel—doing exactly the opposite.

Here is a sobering truth. Most (that is, the overwhelming majority of) Bible-reading, Bible-believing Christians do not know the Bible! This statement is neither intended as an exaggeration, nor by any means a holier-than-thou indictment by an unaffiliated armchair critic. It is indeed, an honest observation of a concerned fellow pilgrim, and a brotherly call for serious self-examination and thoughtful engagement. Yes, many a Bible believer has read the Bible from cover to cover, and not a few has done it many times over. Notwithstanding, the paucity of biblical understanding among avowed Bible believers remain alarmingly pervasive. The Bible is being read and *understood* alright, but in ways not intended by the divine or human authors of the Bible. Rather than being read as the integrated and holistic word of God, it is read and known as segmented collections of chapters and verses. Thus, the Bible is made to succumb to the mercy and fancy of the user, whose prerogative it then becomes to cobble up chapters and verses in any form or order of her or his whims to make whatever points s/he wishes it to make. No thanks to supposedly helpful but potentially harmful Bible study tools and practices such as Bible concordances, topical Bibles, decontextualized daily guides, Bible verse memorization and memory verses; as well as notoriously egregious books of *Bible Promises* and the likes.

This situation is not limited to the pew, but extends also to the pulpit. It explains why a great many Bible practitioners, preachers, pastors, teachers, missionaries, and seminarians do not indeed teach or preach the Bible, but rather preach and teach their ideas of what they think the Bible might be saying. Again, this is not intended as an aloof thumbing of nose at the calling and labor of faithful people of God. Yet, speaking the truth in love, a vast majority of Bible-believing Christians, Bible teachers and preachers approach the Bible as one would approach a well-stocked refrigerator in the morning. One opens the fridge, picks up some tomatoes, onions, and peppers here; eggs, sausages, and bacon there, whip them all up nicely together, toast and, breakfast is served! Another one might as well also come to the fridge, pick up the same ingredients, and whip up something completely different…and breakfast is served! Operating with the selfsame *refrigerator approach* to biblical interpretation, the Bible practitioners alike pick up a verse here, a chapter there, or even a word here and phrase or sentence there, and combine them in whichever way his whimsical "spirit leads" and *voila,* the hermeneutic breakfast is served! While this approach may well serve a variety of our appetites and satisfy our individual culinary preferences, it cannot suffice for the word of God. The way not to know the Bible is to *know* it as chapters and verses.

It is uncertain when the first attempts at divisions, notations and paratexts began to appear in the earliest manuscripts. We have noted earlier that neither God nor the original authors of the Scriptures gave it in chapters and verses. Different kinds of divisions and subdivisions began to appear in the post 2nd Temple period[16] of the Jewish Bible (Tanakh). By the 10th Century AD, these divisions had begun to appear in the Masoretic Text. In about 920 AD, the bounded manuscripts of the Tanakh—*Keter-Aram-Soba* (*Crown of Aleppo* aka *Aleppo Codex) – was written* with such divisions. The divisions were not chapters and verses as we now have them today. They were composed of *parashots,* roughly equal to what today we would refer to as paragraphs. In about 1227 Stephen Langton, Archbishop of Canterbury, developed a system of

---

[16] Historically, 2nd Temple Judaism designates the approximately 600-year period from the return of exiles from Babylon, the rebuilding of the temple in Jerusalem in ca. 516 BC to its destruction in 70 AD.

chapter divisions, which was used 155 years later by the Wycliffe English Bible in 1382. This Langton/Wycliffe pattern of chapter divisions has been largely adopted by Bible publishers to date.

Differing divisions and notations appeared on other codices, including New Testament manuscripts until into the 16th century. In 1448, Rabbi Nathan divided the Tanakh into verses; and in 1555 Robert Estienne (aka Stephanus) mostly adopting Nathan's model, divided the New Testament in the standard numbered verses we have become accustomed to. Five years later in 1560, the Geneva Bible became the first English Bible to be published with chapter and verse divisions as we know it today. Our familiarity with it today notwithstanding, chapters and verses are obviously a very recent additions to the Bible.

If God did not reveal Scriptures in chapters and verses, why then was the Scriptures later divided in the first place? What were the purposes of chapter and verse divisions? We can deduce the original intent of early divisions in the two main methods of division of the early Tanakh—*parashot* and *sedarim*. The *parashot* was thematic while the *sedarim* was based on quantity. Moses had commanded the Torah to be read out aloud before the congregation on the sabbath and festivals (cf. Deuteronomy 31:9f.), and Ezra the scribe, according to Jewish traditions, established the practice of public reading of Torah on Mondays, Thursdays, and Saturdays. The Torah was divided into ca 154 sections (*sedarim*) to be completed in a three-year cycle in ancient times or divided into 54 sections to be read every sabbath and completed every calendar year as in modern Judaism. So, the purpose of *sederim* division was to aid public reading (and completion) of oral Torah. The *parashot* on the other hand is thematic, functioning in a way like a modern paragraph. From the foregoing, we can deduce that the intent of subdivisions in the Bible was to aid comprehension—through audio-visual intake of the entirety of Scriptures and in-depth learning of themes and topics.

How and why then has a good thing turned to the albatross that it has become today? The first part of the problem is that today's Bible readers have gotten so accustomed to seeing the Bible with chapters and verses that they could not imagine the Bible without it. Many wrongly assume that chapters and verses are part of divine inspiration, the way God gave it and the way we must read, understand, and use it. Coupled with the totality of several other misunderstandings about the Bible, some of which we have outlined in this book, they mis/quote, misapply and misuse Bible verses in ways that severely becloud or distort the word of God. More perniciously, this pervasive practice attempts to put words in God's mouth, and make God seem to say what God has not said, or attempt to obligate God into 'fulfilling' promises God never made in the first place.

God watches over his word to perform it (cf. Jere 1:12), but not our misinterpretation of God's word.

And there is no question but that our 'refrigerator' understanding of the Bible in terms of chapters and verses, lead inexorably to misinterpretation and misapplication of the word of God. Imagine how much of 'Bible teachings,' 'revelations,' church 'doctrines,' and even theological traditions that are based on prooftexts derived from misunderstood and misused chapters and verses! Imagine the empty 'promises' we claim, the vacuous 'prophetic' pronouncements, and false hopes we entertain due to our biblical illiteracy! Imagine the cacophony of voices, the unending feuds, the confusion, and the divisions due simply to not receiving, reading, understanding, and applying the Bible as God intended it.

The Christian ideal is to do unto others as you would have them do unto you (cf. Matthew 7:12). Or at the very least, to not do unto others as one would have them not do in return. How often do we hear Bible-believing Christians mouth that the Bible is God's love letter to us? Yet, these same Christians turn around and treat God's 'love-letter' with such utter shabbiness and contempt by chopping it up into bits and pieces, picking and choosing whatever tickles one's itching fancies and fits into however poorly preconceived personal or denominational theological narratives. Who does that or who is that 'lover' that would treat a lover's letter with such disrespect? Who is that lover that would prefer for her/his letter to a dear one be treated that shabbily?!

Which brings us full circle to the question: how then shall we read and understand the Bible? Answer: as God intended it; this is as continuous story without the manmade and artificial breaks of chapters and verses. Keep in mind for the umpteenth time, that the chapters and verses in your Bible are not part of divine revelation. They are, albeit well-intended, artificial, manmade props inserted to help, but now hinder our understanding of God's word. Therefore begin, maybe the first time for some, by reading the Bible as if the chapter and verse divisions were not there. It may warrant your tapping or painting over the chapter and verse divisions—it is worth it! Thankfully, several Bible publishers have begun to publish Bibles without chapters and verses.[17] It is worth investing in these

[17] Biblica, New International Version (NIV); Crossway, English

Bibles, and reading God's word as God intended it to be read.

Take a smaller book—say, one of the epistles of Paul. He has a pattern of writing—usually, here are the *facts* to then, *so what?* That is, from *theology* (basis) to their *implications* for life and conduct (cf. Romans 1:1-11:36, 12:1-16:27; Ephesians 1-3:21, 4:1-6:24). His correspondence were often addressed to his young associates or protégé (cf. 1 Timothy 1:2; Titus 1:4; Philemon 1), or one of his church plants (cf. 1 Corinth. 1:2; Galatians 1:2)—children whom he, as if a woman in labor, had birthed with delirious pain (cf. Galatians 4:19). Observe the introductory remarks and salutation (cf. Colossians

---

Standard Version (ESV); Bibliotheca, American Standard Version (ASV); Independently published, Holy Bible – World English Bible (WEB), Lulu Press, The New Testament Bible Without Chapters or Verses—Chronologically (KJV)

1:1; 1 Thessalonians 1:1). Pay attention to the transitional statements, which often introduce the subject matter or purpose of the correspondence (cf. 1 Corinth. 1:10f.) Take note of and follow the themes, argumentation, and development of theological foundations upon which Paul will base the injunctions (Ephesians 1:1-3:21). Then, finally note and correlate the *so whats?* (Eph. 4:1ff.; Col. 3:1ff.) Move on with other books of the Bible.

The foregoing is obviously not the say that chapters and verses have no place in the Bible. Of course, they do. However, their usefulness will continue to be far dwarfed by the hinderances they pose without first reading and understanding the overarching structure, themes, plot, purpose and message of each text, book, testament, and Bible as a whole. Then and only then can we skillfully use and apply scriptural verses without misquoting and distorting the message of the Bible. As you begin to understand the purposes, themes, argumentation, and conclusions of each book, and piece the chronology of the books of the Bible; you will begin to appreciate in a new way the astonishing beauty, wisdom and majesty of God's word and the God of the word!

Article 6: What The Bible Says Is Not What The Bible Teaches

The Sixth Article of Biblical Understanding states that: What The Bible Says Is Not What The Bible Teaches - meaning is in the whole.

Let the reader understand (Matthew 24:15).

A corollary of our *refrigerator* and *Daily Guide*[18] approach to the Bible is oft repeated "the Bible says…," followed by a triumphant quotation from a verse of Scriptures or the other. The formulaic is ubiquitous in its frequency of usage among Bible believing Christians, and it is often stated with such finality as to freeze all debates or discussions. *'The Bible said it, I believe it, and that settles it!"* So, the refrain goes. But does it? Is it indeed settled because the Bible "said it?" Not so fast, because nothing about the Bible is really settled until it is

[18] See Article #7

settled correctly. When we hear or say "the Bible says...," we need to be mindful of the fact that what the Bible *says* is not the same thing, or as important, as what the Bible teaches. Yes, the Bible may *say* it, but that does not mean that it is what the Bible *teaches*. In fact, the Bible may say something very different or even opposite of what the Bible teaches. In other words, while we hear or loosely use the expression of "Bible says," the meat of biblical understanding is in discovering what the Bible teaches on all subjects of which the Bible speaks. Meaning or message of the text, a book, or the Bible itself is not in individual verses but in the overall text, book, and Bible. Consider this sampling of Bible verses:

"An eye for an eye" *Eye for eye, tooth for tooth, hand for hand, foot for foot,* Exodus 21:24

"Train up a child...and he will not depart from it" *Train up a child in the way he should go; even when he is old he will not depart from it,* Proverbs 22:6.

"Command ye me" *Thus saith the LORD, the Holy One of Israel, and his Maker, Ask me of things to come concerning my sons, and concerning the work of my hands command ye me,* Isaiah 45:11, (KJV).

"Judge not" *Judge not, that you be not judged,* Matthew 7:1.

"Give and it shall be given to you" *Give, and it will be given to you. Good measure, pressed down, shaken together, running over, will be put into your lap. For with the measure you use it will be measured back to you,* Luke 6:38.

"Search the Scriptures" *Search the Scriptures; for in them ye think ye have eternal life: and they are they which testify of me,* John 5:39 (KJV).

"Ye need not that any man teach you" *But the anointing which ye have received of him abideth in you, and ye need not that any man teach you: but as the same anointing teacheth you of all things, and is truth, and is no lie, and even as it hath taught you, ye shall abide in him.* 1 John 2:27 (KJV).

"An eye for an eye" *Eye for eye, tooth for tooth, hand for hand, foot for foot,* (Exodus 21:24). Growing up I frequently heard this "scripture" bandied around. I did not know a whole lot about the Bible, so it was easy to be bamboozled by this relative who as his personal guiding principle believes, according to him, in this "law of Moses." Further recast in local Nigerian pigeon, this revenge principle is expressed as *"do me I do you God no go vex."* I still encounter Christians who either subscribe to the vengeful import of the so-called "law of Moses," or struggle with how to harmonize it with what they instinctively know to be the Christian ethos of forbearance. The first thing worth noting is that Pentateuchal *hammisphatim* (the *decisions* or *judgments*) like the Decalogue itself were not addressed to the individual Israelite, but given as further elaborations of God's covenant with corporate Israel (cf. Exodus 19:3f.; Deuteronomy 5:1f.). There is, in this specific instance, no command, injunctions or authority for an individual Israelite to take it upon him or herself to exert retribution upon another individual on account of personal injury. The prescriptions here—comparable to sentencing guidelines in our modern jurisprudence—were given to magistrates and judges in the dispensation of justice and for societal decorum (cf. Exodus 21:22ff.; Deuteronomy 19:18f). The guidelines serve the precise purpose of curtailing arbitrariness or excessive vengeful impulses. The vital point is that human life is sacred and God's people must treat it as such. There is no requirement or injunction for individual pursuit of revenge. To the contrary the overall tenor of interpersonal relationships in Scriptures is one undergirded by grace and forbearance (cf.

Leviticus 18:18, Duet. Mark 12:31f; 5:38f, Romans 12:19; 13:8f).

"Train up a child... and he will not depart from it" (Proverbs 22:6). Many a parent has been laden with debilitating burden of guilt and shame because of the presence of one wayward child or another, assumed to be proof positive they have fallen foul of God's word. Where did we go wrong, and what could we have done differently to see this Scripture (Proverbs 22:6) fulfilled in the lives of our wayward children? Why is this promise of God not fulfilled for us? What about many Missionary Kids (MKs) and Pastor's Kids (PKs) who are notorious for turning their backs on the faiths of their parents? The first thing to note here is that there is no promise or one-to-one correlation that if a happens

b must follow. The book of *Proverbs* is a form of the category of writings (genre) called Wisdom Literature. *Proverbs,* is a collection of pithy sayings that attempt to explain how things may or do usually happen in the real world, all things being equal. There are a range of factors, including free will, which make it such that even children raised by Godly parents may depart from their parent's faith. Children raised by godly parents in a godly way would most likely follow and not depart from the ways of their parents. Or they may not. As a genre, Proverbs is written and interpreted properly not as promises to be fulfilled, but as how things generally do turn out; but may also turn out differently in specific real-life circumstances.

"Command ye me" (Isaiah 45:11-KJV). Many years ago, we were in a prayer session when this dear ministry colleague was profusely and vociferously going "God, I command you…because you said in your word 'command ye me'." (He is still a better man than me), but I just could not shake the sinking feeling that something was off with that kind of prayer. It was in the Bible sure enough, but it just did not sit comfortably with me commanding God. Neither should it sit well with you, nor should you dare to command God "because the Bible says so." Notice that the quote is a rendition of King James Version of the English Bible, and as we have noted earlier, the KJV suffers from the obsolesce of Jacobian English. Simply read in newer English translation and in context (Article #10), we realize that rather than being an encouragement to do so, it was rather a rebuke for daring to command or question God or God's judgement about the works of his hands!

"Judge not" (Matthew 7:1). "Are you judging…me?" "I am not judging…." One of the cardinal sins today in America, it appears, is making any kind of moral judgement about any person or any person's character or actions. "Are you judging me?" is an instant conversation-stopper. How dare you judge me? to which the addressee scampers into a sheepish 'no not at all, I'm not judging you." This new cardinal sin about not judging is apparently based on the mistaken idea that God forbids judging, as taught in this mis/quotation. First of taken literally, the statement "do not judge" is inherently contradictory and a self-defeating impossibility. The statement has already made a judgement that judging is wrong, and the only way anyone could abide by it is by breaking it and judging that judging is wrong. Secondly, Jesus would be commanding his listeners to violate the very command he is giving by giving them (in the same chapter!) a series of scenarios where they need to make judgement, e.g. vv.5, 6, 13, 14, 21. At least, Jesus is asking his listeners to make self-reflective judgements (log in the eye), personality/quality judgements (person-dogs-pigs), character judgments (false prophets), (outcome judgements (good fruit and bad fruits), authenticity judgement (say-do) etc. Clearly, the Lord is teaching here about destructive and unproductive criticisms and condemnation of others outside of the stipulations he has given. Of such would be the pharisaic traducers of our Lord's day, as well as the holier-than-thou busybodies and "assistant Jesuses" of our day. But there is nothing in the Scriptures that prohibit constructive and necessary critique, factual, value or moral judgments and necessary corrections and appropriate sanctions.

"Give and it shall be given to you" (Luke 6:38). It is in the light of the above the we would also understand this Lukan statement. Notice in the second verse of Matt. 7, the Lord cautions that the judgement (destructive criticism and condemnation) one gave out would also be the kind of return one should expect to receive back. Luke picks up and expands the warning about the payback one gets from a penchant for gratuitous criticisms and insults. Not only do you get it back, but you get far much more than you dish out--good measure, pressed down, shaken together, and running over! Yeah, rather than being an encourage to give anything, it is after all a warning not to give *it*! If we have been misreading this Scripture, it would have stemmed from not identifying scripturally what the *it* is that we should give and not give.

"Search the Scriptures" (John 5:39 - KJV). It is obviously a wonderful thing to read the Bible; and encouraging God's people to diligently search the Scriptures is great. However, this is not what this passage is teaching, and using it as the Lord's command for his people to do Bible study is simply unwarranted. Just like in the Isaiah's "command me" above, again this error comes from uncritical reliance on the outdated English of KJV. In the KJV quoted in full above, the text appears as an imperative—a command to 'search.' This however is translational error. The original word translated "search" is best translated here (taking cognizance of context—Article #10) as indicative rather than imperative. Translated thusly, it would read "you (people) search...." In a why-can't-you-see-it incredulous manner of saying, the Lord is saying to the Pharisees, "how come you habitually search Scriptures because you think you will find life in it, but fail to see that they in fact testify of me?"

"Ye need not that any man teach you" (1 John 2:27 - KJV). Often in the body of Christ, there are sadly, those who glory in their prideful ignorance. Those who also seek to prevent God's people from seeking knowledge from anyone else or anything outside the captivity of their cocooned self-assured, self-validating theological or ecclesiological enclaves. There seems to be a tendency among many preachers who have grown big and famous without the benefit of proper seminary education to find ways to undermine the invaluable imperative of proper biblical and theological education. As a full-fledged son of the church, one who has lived and operated in fullness of the Spirit north of five decades, and one who also has the privilege of advanced biblical and theological training, let me humbly but most forcefully put on record that there is no substitute to quality (properly standardized and accredited) seminary training for the ministry. It is simply an impossibility to fulfill the mandate of *'rightly dividing the word of truth'* without adequate formal biblical training.

As with the "don't judge" case, this you-don't-need-anyone-to-teach-you statement is nonsensical, if taken literally in the way that our brothers and sisters understand and lob it as cudgel against training. It is nonsensical because it is self-contradictory. If the spirit would tell me everything and needed no one to do so, why then, John, will you be wasting your time, and insulting both the Holy Spirit and me? You obviously did not need to tell them me what you just did, because the Holy Spirit would have told me—and you—that I did not need you to tell me. See the absurdity of that understanding? So, what is John teaching?

First and foremost, let us be clear that neither this Epistle of John nor this text was addressed to any individual believer. 1 John was a general epistle addressed to the late 1st Century congregations in Asia Minor. The text does not, therefore, have any direct application to any individual Christian then or now. A splinter group of secessionists had left the church John was supervising in Asia Minor (v. 19); and John needed to assure the faithful remaining that they indeed, not the deserters, were the true followers of Christ. John's statements to these brethren were not feelgood pep talk, but were based on concreate evidence.

There were two tests of true followership: one, ethical (v. 1-11) and the other, theological (vv. 17f). The deserters' action was proof positive they were not true followers of God. By staying, John's listeners had proven themselves as true believers. They have God's seal of anointing as bearers of truth—need not be bordered with refutation of the lies of the deserters about the fundamentals of the faith (*you need no one to teach you*). Nothing in this passage teaches that even John's hearers, not to talk of any other believer anywhere at any time, did not need education because some "holy spirit" will teach them.

'Is it biblical?' This question comes up with frequent regularity and in a variety of accents and tones among Bible believing people. The sentiment behind this question is understandable and worthy. Serious minded, Bible believing Christians care deeply about doing right by God and living in accord with his word. However, the question is often misleading at least on two counts: firstly, it proceeds from and prompts unwarranted assumptions about the nature and sources of Christian truth; and secondly, it presumes to put on the Bible a burden the Bible never meant or promised to carry. The Bible itself helps us to understand that it is *sufficient* but *incomplete* source of Christian truth. Sufficient in that it is totally adequate for the purposes for which it is given; and incomplete in that it does not assume absolute monopoly of all possible facts and truth—not even Christian truth. This might, at first blush, seem as undermining the authority of the Bible, but it is not. For an (not so profound) example, John tells his audience that the gospel that bears his name was not a comprehensive accounting of every act of

Jesus while physically here on earth with the disciples (John 21:25). Not even all his miracles, signs, and wonders (John 20:30). Everything germane to establishing the truth of Jesus' deity and the eternal life which comes by believing in his name was included (John 20:31). Those things excluded must be accessed obviously from other sources than the gospel, for instance.

"Is it biblical?" presumes erroneously that all questions implicated in Christian life and conduct can be answered by appeal to a text of the Bible or another. Not so. Christian truth is derived *biblically* and/or *theologically*. The questions posed by the phenomena the Christian grapples with may be a biblical question or a theological one. (Of course, there are issues of moral conduct - *ethical* questions;

issues of intersections of creative Christian compassion ethic, body health and wholeness - *pastoral* questions; questions of cross-cultural discipling of nations - *missiological* questions; questions of time and space events, narratives, and witnesses - *historical* questions; questions of observable and measurable data and facts - *scientific* questions; etc.).

A *biblical* question is one which may be answered/resolved mostly, if not entirely, by appeal to the text or clear teaching of the Bible—i.e., by accessing and drawing from the content and tenor of the Bible. A *theological* question on the other hand is one which implicates Christian belief, life, and conduct, but cannot be answered or resolved by simple appeal to biblical texts or teaching. In other words, a theological question arises when an issue of Christian concern or interest cannot be resolved by the clear teaching of the Bible alone. Theological questions arise often because the specific concerns or issues were not directly addressed in the Bible.

Resolution of theological questions involves comprehensively drawing from the Bible as a primary source—biblical principles, examples, analogies, inferences; from the history and traditions of the church over the centuries—asking and reviewing how the church has attempted to deal with this or similar concerns in history; from the lived reality of the worshipping community of believers; and reasonable and cohesive thinking through the whys and wherefores of issues and concerns, with keen attentiveness to cultural imperatives. It should be noted that there is overlap between biblical questions and theological questions and their resolutions are not necessarily mutually exclusive domains of Christian truth.

As it usually shakes out, questions, issues or concerns of Christian interests specifically addressed by the Bible are biblical questions; and, questions, issues or concerns not specifically addressed by the Bible are usually theological questions. Questions such as whether Christians may marry, procreate, and raise families are examples of biblical questions, that could be resolved by appeal to clear and specific teaching of the Bible. Questions of whether a particular person may marry, the choice of specific marriage partners, church and/or traditional legitimating of marriage are theological ones, not specifically addressed by the Bible. Questions of divorce and remarriage are mostly biblical questions, but questions about the number of wives a Christian man may marry are theological questions. Responsible Christian citizenship, leadership and active engagement with political and public policy concerns are mostly biblical questions. Questions about partisan political affiliations, specific platforms, candidates for public offices and public policy priorities, are mostly theological ones. Traditional leadership, title taking, burial and marriage rites, widowhood practices, and myriad of issues where church teachings intersect with local cultures cannot usually be resolved by simple appeal to clear teaching of the Bible, hence must be addressed theologically. It is a biblical question whether a

Christian should work and earn a living, but not so whether to work in a specific industry or job—club, brewery, cigarette, atomic bomb factory or as a hangman. The Bible clearly teaches Christian generosity and support of God's people, his church and work, but in vain do we search for specific scriptural teaching about how to give, how much to give and how often to give in the sanctuary or local assembly. That "Christ died" is both a biblically and historically verifiable question. Add "for our sins" and we are thrust into the deep waters of theological exploration. "God is my father" is a profoundly theological statement, unless you mean that God married your mother and they biologically produced you.

There is considerable distance between Bible times and cultures, and the modern times. Obviously, the Bible could not have specifically addressed the ever-evolving questions and concerns associated with living in an ever-evolving world. From work to sports and entertainment. From filial piety to parental care at home or hospice. New technologies, communication ethics, internet, and social media. From artificial intelligence, synthetic biology, to quantum computing. From bioethics, to robotics. Artificial insemination, human cloning, to 'designer babies.' Myriads of existential questions which cannot be answered by simple appeal to specific texts or clear teaching of the Bible. Questions with grave moral implications to which the church must provide unambiguous answers and guidance for living in the world.

As God's special revelation, the Bible is the final authority of Christian truth, and arbiter of *what then shall we believe?* (dogma/doctrine) and *how then shall we live?* (ethics). Christian truth must accord with the teaching and tenor of the Bible, and at the very least not contradict the Bible. Christian truth is not an *either-or* proposition between Bible or theology, but *both-and.* The question 'Is it biblical?' unless narrowly circumscribed to dealing with questions which can only be resolved solely by Bible exegesis and hermeneutics, can be grossly misleading. What the Bible says is not usually what the Bible teaches. The interpreter's task is to discover the meaning and message of the Bible—text, book, testament, and the entirety of the Bible as a cohesive whole. The Bible has primacy as the final authority and arbiter of Christian life and conduct, yet the Bible has not left us with specific answers to every possible question of Christian life and conduct. Questions that lead us to, not just biblical truth, but full-formed Christian truth. The real question, therefore, is not a narrow 'Is it biblical?' The real question is a full-orbed 'Is it Christian truth?' Truth that is biblically faithful, theologically sound, and culturally attentive.

Article 7: The Bible May Be Given For Us, But The Bible Is Not Given To Us

The Seventh Article of Biblical Understanding states that: The Bible May Be Given For Us, But The Bible Is Not Given To Us – give attention to the original author and audience

> *"When your son asks you in time to come, 'What is the meaning of the testimonies and the statutes and the rules that the LORD our God has commanded you?' then you shall say to your son, 'We were Pharaoh's slaves in Egypt. And the LORD brought us out of Egypt with a mighty hand. And the LORD showed signs and wonders, great and grievous, against Egypt and against Pharaoh and all his household, before our eyes. And he brought us out from there, that he might bring us in and give us the land that he swore to give to our fathers. And the LORD commanded us to do all these statutes, to fear the LORD our God, for our good always, that he might preserve us alive, as we are this day. And it will be righteousness for us, if we are careful to do all this commandment before the LORD our God, as he has commanded us'* (Deuteronomy 6:20f.).

> *Now these things happened to them as an example, but they were written down for our*

> *instruction, on whom the end of the ages has come* (1 Corinthians 10:11).

We begin unpacking this rule by reiterating two important points. First, the meaning or message of the Bible—the eternal word of God—is universal and timeless. That is to say that the truths contained in, and conveyed through the Bible always *applies,* to all peoples and in all places. Second, the (text of the) Bible is given through human persons to other living human persons, in specific times and spaces. The distinction between meaning or message and text or form is crucial because while one (the former) is timeless and universal, the other (the latter) is temporal and circumscribed. History involves the recording and recounting of past events and peoples, to a present audience, and preservation of accounts and records for future audiences. The human person through whom God gave the spoken and or the written word we call the *original author.* (We have already discussed the divine-human authorship of the Bible in Article #1, and take as given the Holy Spirit's abiding superintendence of the writing, transmission, and interpretation of Scriptures). The human person/s to whom the word was given in the first instance we call the *original audience.* Especially in historical accounts and records, the persons about whom the original authors spoke or wrote we call the *original characters.* Hence, the text of historical accounts and books often involve original characters, original author, and original audience. These characters together play a critical role in textual interpretation and biblical understanding.

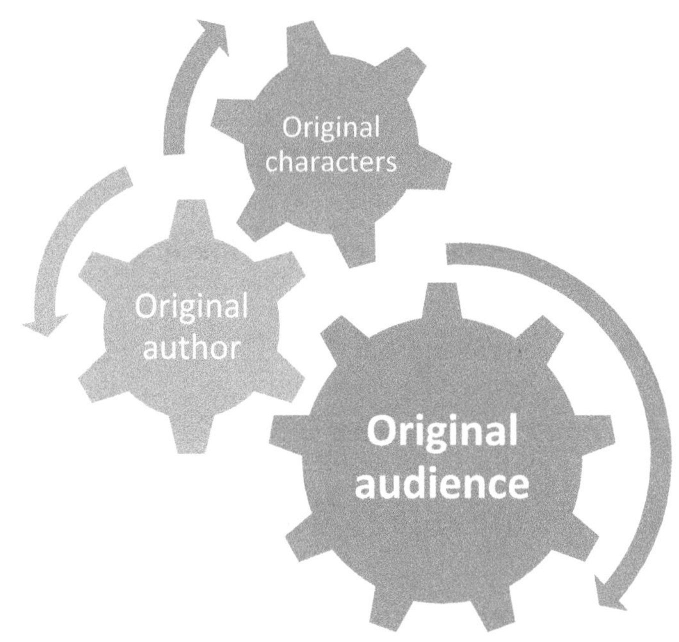

Figure 4 Historical accounts & books: Dramatis personae

Biblical history preserves the mighty acts of God for present and future generations. The Passover was first instituted for Israelites in Egypt as a symbol of God's deliverance (Exodus 12:1ff.). In writing and recounting this event for the wilderness Israelite audience, Moses now codifies the Passover, to be memorialized and commemorated for his present audience, and for yet another future audience. *And when your children say to you, 'What do you mean by this service?' you shall say, 'It is the sacrifice of the LORD's Passover, for he passed over the houses of the people of Israel in Egypt, when he struck the Egyptians but spared our houses.'"* (Exodus 12:26, 27). Note that Moses (the original author) was here recounting and commemorating this event which took place several years earlier among the exodus Israelites (original characters), now being codified and memorialized for the (present) post-exodus wilderness generations of Israelites (original audience) and for future generations, as a constant reminder of God's mighty acts in (their) history. In the Old Testament Deuteronomic passage (quoted above) the codification and memorialization of the *"testimonies and the statutes and the rules that the*

LORD our God has commanded" them served a slightly enlarged role as rationale for commanding their obedience. The Divine Suzerain always reserves the right of sovereignty over vassal Israel by past acts of deliverance (*"the LORD brought us out of Egypt with a mighty hand"),* present protection and fulfilment of promise (*"that he might bring us in and give us the land that he swore to give to our fathers"),* and for future preservation (*"for our good always, that he might preserve us alive"*). Thus, God's deliverance of Israel from Egyptian captivity constitutes a powerful basis for the covenant promises, obligations, and sanctions.

In New Testament 1 Corinthians, Apostle Paul was confronting yet another audience, different from that of Moses and the reader today. According to the text, Paul (the original author, cf. 1:1), was addressing the Corinthian believers-recipients (the original audience, cf. 1:2)), about those he variously referred to as "our fathers" (cf. 10:1), "all," "they," "them," throughout the text (the original characters, cf. 10:1-11), and events which took place several thousand years prior during the post-exodus wilderness wandering. Here, Paul reveals to his Corinthian contemporary audience, the purpose of documenting and preserving, for posterity, the faithless acts of their fathers and the consequences.

The motley crown of Israelites who marched out of Egyptian bondage towards the promised land had tested and stretched the patience of both Moses and God to breaking points. In diverse ways at various junctures, they had experienced the awesome power of God on their behalf, and been direct beneficiaries of God's providential lovingkindness. Despite all that and through it all, their faithless whining, and complaining and doubts about the viability of the promised land progressed nonstop. Their unfaith reached depths of demeaning idolatrous practices. *And they rose up early the next day and offered burnt offerings and brought peace offerings. And the people sat down to eat and drink and rose up to play* (Exodus 32:6). There were unsuccessful attempts to subvert the people and return to Egyptian bondage. *Nevertheless, with most of them God was not pleased, for they were overthrown in the wilderness* (1 Corinthians 10:5). Korah's unsuccessful coup against the leadership of Moses had attracted God's judgment resulting in the death of some 14,950 souls (cf. Numbers 16:1f.). Their unholy dalliance with Baal Peor would result in 24,000 deaths (Numbers 25:1f.)! Their unfaith would come to a head when God would vow to wipe out that entire offending exodus generation in forty years of wilderness perambulation, and start anew with the children they had so worried about (cf. Number 14:26f.). From the Old Testament records of these people and events, Paul had drawn object lessons for his contemporary Corinthian audience.

The Bible reader or preacher today confronts and interacts with the text of the Bible as a distant third person. In each text of Scriptures, s/he interacts usually with original characters, an original author, and original audience. The today's Bible reader or preacher is neither the original character, nor the original author nor the original audience. In some instances, especially where texts of Scriptures—say the Old Testament—is used by New Testament writers, a text may contain more than one set each of characters and audiences. This is not only true of this text (cf. 1 Corinthians 10:1f.), but also in other texts and narratives of the Bible. The lessons of the specific referenced texts belong to us Bible readers today, after all we could still possibly be part of those *"on whom the end of the ages has come,"* (v.11b). However, we today are not the original characters, we are not the original audience, and we sure are not the original authors of the texts or books of the Bible. Bible revelation was not given to us today's readers as direct audience. For that same reason we should never read the Bible (or verse, text, or book of the Bible) today as if it were given to us as direct recipients. To do so will lead inexorably to misreading of Scriptures.

Habits, of course, die hard. It must be acknowledged that we have perfected a lifetime of reading the Bible in a certain, albeit wrong, way. A sanitized version of the opening lines of (otherwise profanity-laced) song "Kwaku the Traveler,"[19] might read something like:

> *"Of course, I flubbed up;*
> *Who never flubbed up?*
> *Hands in the air;*
> *No hands…*

Kwaku's *mea culpa* may seem more of a cop out than genuine admission of guilt, but it is safe to say that all us at some point or other read the Bible as it were given to us directly. The habit might probably

---

[19] 2022 hit single by Ghanaian artiste: Black Sherif, real name Mohammed Ismail Sherif Kwaku Frimpong

be widespread and extends from pew to pulpit, and from quiet time to outdoor preaching. Kwaku invites his audience to own up to their mistakes, learn from them, dust themselves up and keep on running the race of life. We learned to read the Bible wrongly. It will take some unlearning and relearning to read it right. Whether or not we can stretch the *"whom the end of the ages has come"* in 1 Corinthians 10:11 or some ambiguous passages to include today's readers is beside the main point. The key point is that Bible (in whole or parts) involves original authors, original audiences, and (in most cases) original characters, which are not us today's readers. The Bible is given *for* us—for our benefit, for our guidance, for our encouragement, for our instruction, for our correction in righteousness. As God's truth the Bible's import always extends to all peoples. However, the Bible is not given *to* us—we are not the original recipients of the written word. When we read any text or book of the written word today, we must never assume to read it as if the Bible speaks to us directly as the original recipients. We must read by paying close attention to the original characters, the original audiences, and the original authors.

Article 8: You Are Not Always The "You" In The Text

The Eighth Article of Biblical Understanding states that: You Are Not Always The "You" In The Text - it often refers to original audience

> *And you Philippians yourselves know that in the beginning of the gospel, when I left Macedonia, no church entered into partnership with me in giving and receiving, except you only. Even in Thessalonica you sent me help for my needs once and again. Not that I seek the gift, but I seek the fruit that increases to your credit. I have received full payment, and more. I am well supplied, having received from Epaphroditus the gifts you sent, a fragrant offering, a sacrifice acceptable and pleasing to God. And my God will supply every need of yours according to his riches in glory in Christ Jesus. To our God and Father be glory forever and ever. Amen.* (Philippians 4:15-20).

Recently, I stumbled upon an Instagram[20] video. A man was testifying and urging upon his listeners a prayer he said his dad had taught him. The prayer, he proclaimed, "broke the curse of poverty," and

---

[20] "Prayer To Change Your Financial Trajectory," accessed August 17, 2023.

"brought extreme blessings" on his family. Narrating the story of his family life, the man talked about how he "grew up supper poor." So poor that there were days they did not have anything to eat. His dad, he said, "was an evangelist," and they "lived in a trailer." They "were completely broke." His dad "prayed this prayer that changed [their] family's financial trajectory forever." The prayer his dad taught him, he now prayed thus:

> Father, you said in your word that you will supply all our needs according to your riches in glory by Christ Jesus. God, this job isn't our source, this government isn't our source. God, you have the ability to provide multiple streams of income, miraculously…
>
> God, I speak in the name of Jesus…that you're working behind the scenes right now to activate their preferred financial future. Their struggling days are over, and hope is coming…

> God, I speak this over their lives, financial breakthrough, in Jesus' name, amen!

He then proceeded to urge his listeners to "share with five people," save, and continue to pray it, "over and over…because [most assuredly] it works!" And without a doubt it will work for them.

The prayer and the sentiment fomenting it obviously stem from the presumed "promise" which God, supposedly, made to *us* in Philippians 4:19. *And my God will supply every need of yours according to his riches in glory in Christ Jesus.* Not only is there a presumption of promise to claim, but there is also a concomitant presumption of that promise being made directly to us as readers today. Both presumptions as presumptions often go, are indeed false. There is no promise made by anyone to anyone in this passage, and nothing addressed directly to the Bible reader today. In the immediate previous discussion of Article #7, we have encountered the three parties to a biblical text—original characters, original author, and original audience—aside from a fourth party, i.e., the reader today. In its original form, the written word of God was given through real life human persons, and addressed to other real-life persons, about real-life persons, and events, in specific contexts. While the Bible reader today may be a direct recipient of the *message*, s/he is not the direct recipient of the words of the Bible (see especially also, Article #9, #12). There are, of course, the "whosever' type passages which may carry direct universal imports, but the overwhelming bulk of the written word—commands, promises, etc.—were addressed directly to original audiences apart from today's Bible reader.

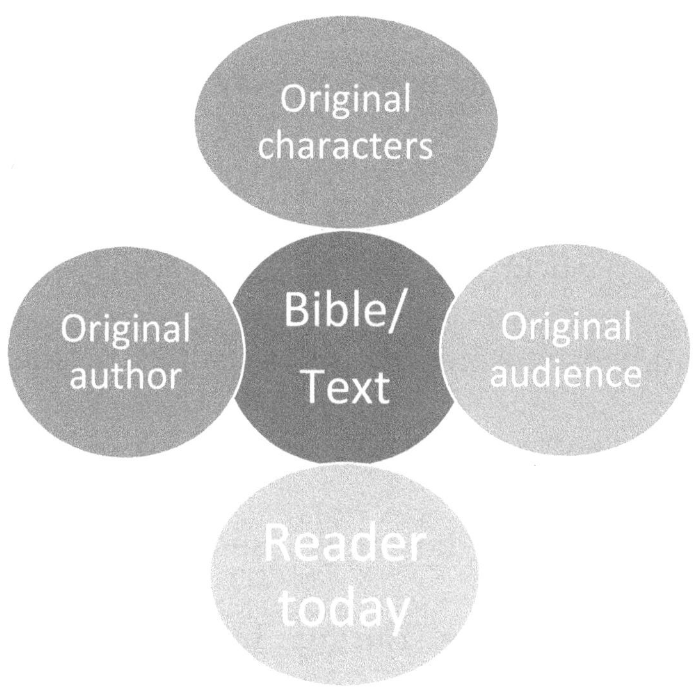

Figure 5 Parties to Bible/Text

God will supply all your needs? Maybe, but the textual context (Article #10) of Philippians 4:15 show that the statement of this verse was neither a promise, nor was the non-promise directed at the Bible reader today. God definitely can, and whether God wills to supply all your needs is beside the point here. In the passage under review "yours" simply does not mean yours, the Bible reader. At this point it should already be clear that "yours" refer immediately to those of the original audience (cf. Article #7, above). The addressees (original audience) were *"the saints in Christ Jesus who are in Philippi"* (v.1). Those were the Apostle's benefactors-in-need, who alone supported him during a trying time during his missionary endeavors out of Macedonia (cf. v. 15;). In a heartfelt "thank you" moment, Paul wrote to express a desire, not a promise, offering a prayer that his missionary God would attend to their own needs in the same way they had attended to his.

Clearly, the message of this text can be summarized in the simple maxim that *one good turn deserves another.* God's work, evangelistic and cross-cultural disciple-making work in particular, requires and deserves the sacrificial support of God's people. And those who support the work of missions and God's global agenda, could expect the missionaries' reward—which obviously would not be cash, but like Paul here, a heartfelt prayer for God's equitable reward. Insofar as it is offered from a worshipful disposition and not simply as that well-worn manipulative, *quid pro quo,* money-doubling "giving" scheme, we may indeed pray for the blessings of Philippians 4:19, as accompaniment of our reasonable sacrifice of support of genuine cross-cultural kingdom work. It is instructive that Paul—easily the greatest Apostle to have ever lived—did not have enough financial resources to take care of even his own basic needs, but depended on the benevolence of willing fellow believers. How blasphemous of many a "great men and women of God," and many more modern "prosperity gospel[21], " "prophetic" and "faith" practitioners to twist Paul's missions-infused prayers in the merchandizing of the "gospel" and for filthy lucre?! The many well-intentioned Christians who have fallen for "claiming" this non-promise "promise" that no one made to anyone in the first place, based

---

[21] "...the teaching that faith—expressed through positive thoughts, positive declarations, and donations to the church—draws health, wealth, and happiness into believers' lives. It is also referred to as the "health and wealth gospel" or "name it and claim it." Central to this teaching are the beliefs that salvation through Jesus Christ includes liberation from not only death and eternal damnation but also poverty, sickness, and other ills. Adherents believe that God wants believers to be richly blessed in this life and that physical well-being and material riches are always God's will for the faithful. Illness and poverty are seen as curses that, through atonement, can be broken with faith in Jesus." Encyclopedia Britannica, Britannica.com, accessed Nov. 2023.

simply on false assumptions! And, the much more Bible-believing Christians who "claim" biblical promises because it has a "you," "us," and the like. How lazy and irresponsible of some preachers who encourage their audiences to "put your name" in such or such scriptural verses on the preposterous presumption that doing so will somehow cause God to misunderstand His own word?!

Without doubt, the Bible teaches prosperity. After all, the manward purpose of God in creation and redemption is *human flourishing,* or what our Lord speaks of as *"life…abundantly"* (John 10:10). However, biblical flourishing is grander, profounder, much more holistic, and virtuous than greed-suffused hedonistic materialism. And most "prosperity preachers" and merchants of "faith" will go out of business tomorrow, were the Bible to be interpreted, understood, and taught properly. Someone may retort with, as our Instagram preacher said, "but *it works!*" And, therein lies a real danger in these kinds of abuse of God's word—even if it only seems to work. For when the will of God is available and accessible, even a "glorious" end can never justify a contrary means. One might question: "what about our experiences," our "what I have tested and proven," our "in my personal walk with the Lord," etc.? In our discussion of Article #6, we had noted that the individual and corporate living and lived experience of God's people is a key funder of Christian truth. Our personal and collective experience of the changed lives and active or renewed obedience to God is a key *verifier* of the biblical truth of the new birth.

The Apostle Jacob taught as much when he argued that faith (as belief) that is not coupled with active works of righteousness is practically ineffectual (James 2:14ff.). *"Isn't it obvious that God-talk without God-acts is outrageous nonsense?"* he asked in the seventeenth verse.

The experience of the individual Christian or corporate body of Christ may be a validator of what is believed to be true. It is, however, critically important to recognize and understand that experience cannot sustain itself as self-authenticating and self-validating source of truth. Human experiences are pervasive and variegated. We see things differently. Not even members of the same family or congregation, experience the same phenomenon the same way. The presence of unexplained phenomena, a supernatural occurrence, a "miracle," or "answers to prayer," do not necessarily mean they are unexplainable or that God is at work. Opinions vary and many times contradict, and contradicting opinions cannot both be true. Our experience must accord with, and be validated by, some higher independent authority. Experiences, no matter the effect or vividness, must submit to that higher verifying authority, the Bible—properly interpreted. God's truth stands in judgment over experience, and not vice versa. It is the written word of God, not the individual or collective experience of believers, denominations, or church, that is the final authority in matters of Christian life and conduct.

"Wait, did Paul not place experience (demonstration of power) over *words* when he made the statement to the effect that his speech and message were '*not in plausible words of wisdom, but in demonstration of the Spirit and of power,*'" (1 Corinthians 2:4)? Glad you asked? Again, we should already by now have some answers for the question. For starters, the Apostle was speaking specifically about his entrance among his Corinthian audience. Secondly, Paul was not saying that his "demonstration of spirit and power" were of themselves self-validating authority, but rather that the experience helped to validate his "speech and message." Moreover, *plausible words of wisdom* (*enticing words of man's wisdom* – KJV) is not a reference to the word of God, but an obvious reference to Greek rhetoric—analogous to the theological summersaults and lingual gymnastics many adopt in selling untutored ideas of what the Bible is supposed to teach and pet "revelations." As we have already discussed in Article #5, Paul was a systematic teacher of the word with discernible method of teaching and writing. Review of his writings indicate a teaching strategy of injunctions and commandments grounded on solid biblical and theological understanding—i.e., whys - wherefores, truth - implications, theology - conduct. It is deceptive and reckless to selectively amass a hodgepodge of Pauline (or for that matter, biblical) verses such as this to teach or imply that our experiences can in any way trump the primacy of (clear teaching of) the word of God.

Of course, the Bible contains generic statements and promises of God which can be said to potentially belong and directly apply universally to all of God's people. It should be stressed that such universals are exceptions rather than the rule. Scriptural statements, commands, instructions, promises, obligations, and sanctions were often directed at specific persons and audiences. "You" in the Bible rarely, if ever, means you. Genuine appreciation of the authority of Scriptures, sincere quest for scriptural truth, coupled with careful engagement of proper skills and tools of biblical interpretation, will lead us to responsible discernment about what belongs and what does not.

A work of this nature and size can only point with limited examples and comments to the unbelievable array of scriptural verses erroneously quoted and "claimed" out of context simply because they have a "you," "thou," "thee," "your," "yours," or "thy," and thine" on it. The assumption being that they must refer to the reader. The following sampling are, however, offered with the hope that they might help the reader begin to rethink those assumptions and engage in a process of careful reading and understanding and applying the Bible on its own terms. We shall touch on, but leave open the full exploration of how the timeless truths and promises embedded in these words may apply to us as readers today. In other words, the message of these passages—the lessons a reader may derive from them. As a starting point, we reiterate that none of these passages is addressed directly to the reader today.

Bless you and make your name great. *And I will make of* **you** *a great nation, and I will bless* **you** *and make* **your** *name great, so that* **you** *will be a blessing. I will bless those who bless* **you**, *and him who dishonors* **you** *I will curse, and in* **you** *all the families of the earth shall be blessed."* Genesis 12:2, 3). The referent (addressee— "you" or "your") of this passage is the patriarch, Abraham. We notice, thus far and later in Scriptures) the pattern of God's callings and assignments: when/where God calls and gives assignments, he provides the resources and enablement to carry them through to completion. God calls Adam and assigns the cultural mandate of creating a family and beginning civilization, provides him with creation, and especially the complemental other (female). Continuing here, God calls Abraham with the assignment of *"blessings the whole family of the earth,"* and resources him with nation, name, honor, and blessings. The essential message of the text is that God can be trusted to provide the resources for His assignments and tasks.

Lend, be head and not the tail. *And the LORD will make **you** the head and not the tail, and **you** shall only go up and not down, if **you** obey the commandments of the LORD your God, which I command **you** today, being careful to do them,* Deuteronomy 28:13). This is one of the covenant "blessings: declaratives of the Covenant between Yahweh and Israel. The addressee is the congregation of Israel. It was a corporate declaration and always has a corporate import. It was not a promise made to individual Israelites, as evidently some individual Israelites have been *"head"* or *"tail"* throughout history without this covenant declaration being nullified. That the called-out peole of God—the ecclesia—should be assured of God's covenantal trustworthiness, and readiness to reward obedience to God's words is the message of the text.

Never leave or forsake you. *Be strong and courageous. Do not fear or be in dread of them, for it is the LORD your God who goes with **you**. He will not leave **you** or forsake **you**."* Deuteronomy 31:6). This was part of Moses' farewell speech *"to all Israel"* *(**"you"**)* at his 120th birthday; and preparatory towards Joshua's succession (cf. vv1,7). A transitional and, potentially perilous, time. Again, a text with corporate tenor and intent. Clearly, its message of divinw presence, providential faithfulness, stability and trustworthiness—especially during periods leadership transitions is congregational and corporate-directed.

A thousand shall fall at your side...but not come near you. *A thousand may fall at **your** side, ten thousand at **your** right hand, but it will not come near **you**.* Psalms 91:7). This Psalm is a little trickier, because the one "*who dwells in the shelter of the Most High*" could refer to a generic anyone if not a self-reference of the Psalmist's. Whichever the case, it calls attention to our not willy-nilly assuming that once a "you" appears in the Bible, we must rush to assume it is a direct reference to which we could simply put our name. Note also that Psalms is one of the books of poetic literature genre. As such, its interpretation and application differ from say prose or prophecy.

Fear not, for I am with you. *...fear not, for I am with **you**; be not dismayed, for I am* your *God; I will strengthen* you, *I will help* you, *I will uphold you with my righteous right hand.* Isaiah 41:10). Again, the "you" here is not individualistic. As soon as we identify the "you" in this passage as Isaiah's far-sighted vision for post-exilic returnee Israel (cf. vv.8,9), its message and application becomes clearer.

Riches of the Gentiles. *But **ye** shall be named the Priests of the LORD: men shall call **you** the Ministers of our God: **ye** shall eat the riches of the Gentiles, and in their glory shall **ye** boast yourselves*. (Isaiah 61:6 (KJV). This must probably be the source of the outrageous teaching of "wealth transfer." The idea being that some kind of principles, prayers and "prophetic declarations" will somehow move the material wealth of non-believers into the hands and pockets of believers. There is just so much wrong about the thinking behind these kinds of teachings. We will note that referents ("ye") is corporate, and refers to the Israelites of the messianic age. Gentiles are non-Jews, not non-believers. Unwarranted "spiritualizing" of Israel, and scriptural references should not be taught to replace or expunge the *natural branches* (Romans 11:17f,) from the tree of our faith. The passage forms part of a larger rubric of God;s promise of full restoration for Jews in the messianic age; and we non-jews can learn a lesson or two about the abiding nature of God's covenantal commitment *"to a thousand generations"* (cf. Deuteronomy 7:9).

Thoughts I think of you. *For I know the thoughts that I think toward **you**, saith the LORD, thoughts of peace, and not of evil, to give **you** an expected end.* Jeremiah 29:11 (KJV) The direct recipients of Jeremaih's missive within which these words were contained were (Babylonian) exilic Israelites. In the midst of feel-good, gain-without-pain 'prophetic' pronouncements of mealy mouthed 'prophets,' Jeremiah pens a prophesy of divine chastening, endurance and encouragement to exilic Israel. The captivity will take its course, but God would not have forgotten His people. We could learn from this correspondence God's enduring care and concern for His people even at the lowest point of their sin, judgment and exile.

Tread on scorpions and serpents...drink deadly poison. *Behold, I have given* ***you*** *authority to tread on serpents and scorpions, and over all the power of the enemy, and nothing shall hurt* ***you****.* Like the Great Commission and several of such mandates, these statements here and related passages (Luke 10:19, cf. Mark 16:18, Luke 10:10, Mark 16:18) were Jesus' addresses to his assembled first disciples—*ecclesia*. There is no mandate here for an individual discipline to march out stomping away on scorpions and snakes. Anti snake venoms could be very expensive. Again, a corporate promise to the body, and hence, the church has the Lord's assurance of His abiding presence and protection against potential harm and danger.

Prosper and be in good health. *Beloved, I wish above all things that* ***thou*** *mayest prosper and be in health, even as* ***thy*** *soul prospereth.* 3 John 2 (KJV). Like our Philippians 4:19 above discussed, 3 John 2 was a prayer, and not a promise. It was a prayer by the "Elder" (most likely the Apostle John himself) for the health and wellbeing of his beloved son in the lord, Gaius (v1). The message of the passage can teach lessons in honor, respect for elders and rewards of such honor.

Once again, we must note that the truth (meaning and message) of these words as well as others endure forever—as word of God. In the following Articles #9, 10, & 12, we shall discuss the "how to" of making meaning out of the text of Scriptures. Meanwhile, take seriously that the words of Scripture do not apply to us readers today directly as if we were the original audience. You are not the "you" in them. And, we should not read and apply them directly as if they do. The word "you" in them normally refers to the original character/s and audience/s. To read, interpret and understand the Bible properly, we must give attention to the original characters and audiences.

Article 9: The Text Means Nothing To You Until It Means Something Aside From You

The Nineth Article of Biblical Understanding states that: The Text Means Nothing To You Until It Means Something Aside From You - meaning is independent of application.

> *And Ezra opened the book in the sight of all the people, for he was above all the people, and as he opened it all the people stood. And Ezra blessed the LORD, the great God, and all the people answered, "Amen, Amen," lifting up their hands. And they bowed their heads and worshiped the LORD with their faces to the ground. Also…the Levites, helped the people to understand the Law, while the people remained in their places. They read from the book, from the Law of God, clearly, and they gave the sense, so that the people understood the reading* (Nehemiah 8:5-8).

Is there a meaning in a Bible text, a book of the Bible, or the Bible itself? Does the Bible, a book, or text have a determinable meaning and message independent of the reader? If there is meaning in a text, with whom does it reside? With the author?

With the reader? Or somewhere else? These are not just academic questions reserved for scholars and researchers within the four walls of the academy. They are, indeed, questions that confront us all us whenever we open and read the Bible; and which have spiritual and practical consequences for time and eternity.

Most Bible-believing readers, if not all, will disagree with, or disavow the various postmodernist *reader-response*[22] theories about text and interpretation, in which the text possesses no inherent meaning except as supplied by the reader. They would very readily accent to what could be referred to as mainstream orthodoxy, which understands the

---

[22] The theory maintains that textual meaning occurs within the reader in response to text and recognizes that each reader is situated in a particular manner that includes factors such as ability, culture, gender, and overall experiences.

crucial function of author's intention—*authorial intention*—in determining the meaning of a text. Not many, if any at all, will argue against the proposition that the author of the Scriptures—at least to the extent the author is understood as God (the Holy Spirit) himself—communicated through the written word what he intended to communicate. Neither would there be much argument about the fact that the original audience understood what God intended to and did communicate through the original author. Nonetheless, these same believers may turn around and read the Bible as the postmodernist reader-response deconstructionists who insist that meaning resides with the reader[23]

---

[23] U.S. American literary theorist, Stanley Fish, for instance, believes that the meaning of a text is not inherent in the text itself, but is instead constructed by the reader in the act of reading. Those interested in further and more scholarly discussion about hermeneutics, literary theories and deconstructionism may see Keven Vanhoozer's *Is There Meaning*

would do. The irony seems lost on them, insisting on the twin propositions of authorial intention and meaning in a text, on one hand; and on the other hand, turning around in practice to reading and interpreting Scriptures as if the author is irrelevant and the only pertinent meaning of a text is whatever the reader makes of it. Hence, the reader goes through Bible with preemptive intent to find "what the verse/text means to me/us," and with nonchalant regard to what the original author had

---

in the Text? In the work, Vanhoozer engages modern literary theorists, postmodernist deconstructionist thinkers—Jacques Derrida, Michael Foucault, Stanley Fish and Richard Rorty—who tend to deny that any given text could be interpreted and understood with any degree of certainty. In contrast to what he calls "anarchic interpretation" such as the so-called reader-response schema, Vanhoozer believes that "the most important question for contemporary theories of interpretation, whether the Bible or any other book: Is there something in the text that reflects a reality independent of the reader's interpretive activity or does the text reflect only the reality of the reader?" To that question, he answers with a resounding "yes," and suggest a trinitarian hermeneutic third way of reading and interpreting scriptures that not only makes meaning possible, but also leads to its discovery.

intended to communicate—what the text means in and of itself.

The basic assumption of this book is that a biblical text or book of the Bible has identifiable meaning independent of the reader; and that the reader's primary function is to first discover that meaning, and then to secondarily apply or communicate its message to self or others. The original biblical writers chose to select materials, and organized them in particular ways and in particular languages, to communicate messages to particular audiences. The today's Bible reader's primary task is making appropriate effort, using all appropriate means to determine the meaning and message of a text. The reader does not determine the meaning devoid of what the author had intended to convey.

Determining the meaning of the text is a first-order task of biblical interpretation, and determining authorial intention is key to determination of the text's meaning. The question *what the text means,* in and of itself, takes precedence over the secondary question of *what the text means to/for us* readers today.

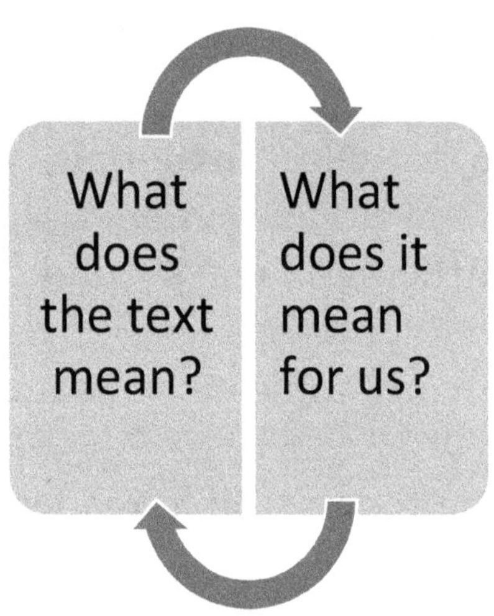

The task of discovering the meaning and message of Scriptures, and contemporizing for newer generations is exemplified in the Nehemiah passage quoted above. After seventy years of Babylonian exile and obviously starved of it, the returnee Jews were all too eager for the *torah.* They requested of the scribe Ezra to fetch the Scroll of the Law of Moses (cf. Deuteronomy 28:61)—the commandments God had given to Moses over nine hundred years earlier. This Ezra brought and read to the assembly of men, women, and children—*all who could understand what they heard*—from dawn till noon. As important as the reading and hearing of the Law, if not more so, the Levites moved in to help teach and make plain the meaning and message of the Law to the people's understanding. *They read from the book, from the Law of God, clearly, and they gave the sense, so that the people understood the reading (Nehemiah 8:8).* This reading, clarifying, and making sense or meaning of the text, and helping the people to understand and apply its message remains still the primary function of the Bible preacher today.

We should be careful to note the crucial difference and the relationship between *interpretation* and *application* of the text of Scriptures. One task is related to the other, but both are distinct one from another. Interpretation of text deals with the process of determining what the text of Scriptures means, i.e., essentially determining what the text meant to the original characters, author, and audience. The fancy word is exegesis, and deals with issues of language, contexts and methods of texts and explanations. The average reader may lack the requisite tools and competency for serious or extensive exegesis, but which should not preclude genuine effort towards correct biblical interpretation and understanding. At a minimum, interpretation asks and answers the twin questions about what the original author intended to convey to the original audience by the written text; and, what the original audience understood the original author to have conveyed by what he wrote.

Application, on the other hand, deals with questions of contemporizing and teasing out principles, inferences, and lessons for life and conduct. Take again, for example, the short text of Genesis 12:1-4. Reckoning with the context (cf. Article #10, below), we note the unstable wilderness setting of the wandering Israelite audience, *vis a vis* the mandate to march through fortified enemy territories across the Jordan and conquer Canaan.

We get a glimpse into their unfaith and self-doubt about their capacity and chances in relation to these peoples (cf. Numbers 13:33; 14:1f.). They were not shy of projecting their weakness and unfaithfulness on God, doubting God's ability and willingness to keep His covenantal promise about the land, and resulting in God's harsh recompense of their unfaith (cf. Numbers 14:11f.). Furthermore, we reckon with the constant urging upon them to be "strong and courageous" (Deuteronomy 11:8; 31:6). All considered, we conclude that Moses' authorial intention, at least in part, would have been to reassure them of God's faithfulness, reaffirm and reestablish their connectedness with both the patriarch Abraham and the enduring covenant with Almighty Yahweh. Assurance of Yahweh's promise-keeping faithfulness preserves God's truth, stabilizes, and sustains them in their present dire wilderness wandering circumstances, and gives them renewed hope for the conquest and occupation of the promised land.

Whenever discernible, the occasion of writing—such as Moses' writing of the Pentateuch during the post-exodus wilderness period—sheds a good deal of light on the text. In retelling the story of Abraham and the other Pentateuchal stories of creation and God's mighty acts to the wilderness generation, both Moses and his audience were reckoning with the sovereign power and faithfulness of the covenant-keeping God. From our vantage point as readers today, we see even more clearly the mighty acts of God and His covenant-keeping faithfulness not only in Abraham but also through the history of his offspring—against otherwise insurmountable odds. This message of divine might and faithfulness the reader today contemporizes and applies as s/he lives to trust and obey the same covenant-keeping promise-keeping God of Abraham, Moses, and the Israelites. Moreover, God's promise to Abraham is already in the past, having been fulfilled completely—in blessings, in name, in both natural and spiritual offspring. Christians believe they are the spiritual children of Abraham, and therefore, the probable fulfillment of God's (*offspring as the stars of heaven*) promise to Abraham (cf. Genesis 22:17; Exodus 32:13). Of all people, Christians ought not be among those who still erroneously "claim" Abraham's blessing by cherry-picking those verses of the Bible, knowing that the Scripture has already been fulfilled, and they are part of its fulfilment!

Of necessity, interpretation must proceed primarily and independent of application. A verse or text of Scripture means nothing to you the reader until it meant something aside from you. The textual meaning is independent of and controls its application to the reading individual and/or community of saints. What the text would have meant to the original author and audience must come first before what the text would mean to me or to us. What the Bible means in and of itself is public truth but its application may be personal. Biblical truth may be personal but never private. It is not subject to individual, parochial, or private inspiration—not even so-called "spiritual impulses" of an interpreter. Otherwise, anarchy pervades and it is every-man-to-himself interpretive free-for-all. The underlying presupposition of our non-anarchical approach to the text/Bible is that the Scriptures possess objective meaning independent of what the reader brings. To that end, the task of the Bible reader/interpreter is to firstly discover the independent meaning of the text; and to then contemporize that meaning/message for oneself and/or others.

So, how shall we approach the interrogation of a scriptural text which leads to determining meaning? What first steps questions shall we ask of the text? With full cognizance of the cruciality of original authors,' original audiences' and characters' intentions and perceptions as meaning-making centers of the text, we first inquire as to the independent meaning of the text prior to its application to contemporary audience/s. What does the text mean? What does it mean for me/us today? Again, the first question is distinct from and logically precedes the second one in that order. Addressing the first question about a text's independent meaning naturally leads to three cognate sub questions: What did it mean to the original characters? What did it mean to the author? and What did it mean to the original audience?

What did it mean to the original characters? The original characters were the persons—human and spiritual—who were active participants in the drama of the text in question. Biblical narratives and chronicles often re/tell accounts of past events to a newer audience who themselves were no part

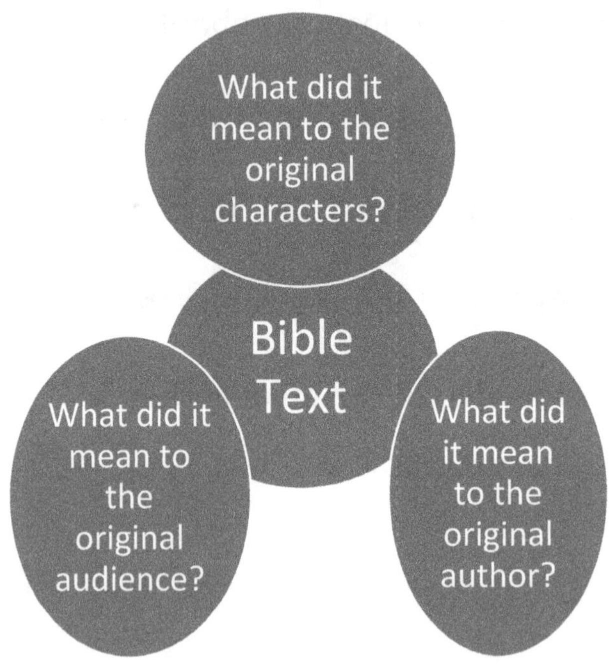

Figure 6 Interrogating Text of the Bible

of the original action. In the Old Testament, much of these is found in the first five books of the Bible

(Pentateuch), the Historical Books from Joshua through the kings, to exilic and postexilic Prophets and chronicles. In the New Testament much of the narrative accounts appear in the Acts and the Gospels. Essential to discovering what a text of the Bible might mean is inquiring and exploring, to the extent possible, who the original characters were, the world they lived in, and what they saw, heard, and felt in real-time.

What did it mean to the original author? An author usually has a purpose or goal for his or her writing. The author conveys this intent—authorial intent—through language and other symbols. This is true of texts whether secular or sacred. An author first determines what message s/he intends to pass on, then selects and organizes materials to enable her/him reach that end. We see this in many books of the Bible, and some texts too. We had encountered this in Proverbs as well as Gospels according to Luke and John. Textually in 1 Timothy 2:1f (more in Article #10, below), the Apostle Paul states the *telos* or goal of his injunction to the Ephesian believers in verse 2 *…that we may lead a peaceful and quiet life, godly and dignified in every way."* In other cases, the intent might not be that clearly stated. In the books and texts where the intent or teleological thrust is not as clearly stated, intent is to be determined by internal and external context of text or book (Article #10, below). Largely, authorial intent controls the way a text should be interpreted, and it is therefore, key to properly guiding the reading and preaching of a text or a boowhoseverk of the Bible. This is not to preclude the possibility of drawing additional lessons than strict adherence to author's intent. It is, however, not rightly dividing the word of truth to ignore it completely, or so deviate from authorial intent as to distorted it.

What did it mean to the original audience? Scriptures were communicated to real-life human persons in real-life circumstances and situations. The authors employed commonly shared languages and cultural symbols to communicate the message of Scriptures in clearly understandable ways. Their writings followed common rules of literature, grammar, and syntax. The Bible was written to be read and understood by all. It is instructive that the Greek of the New Testament was the everyday street *koine*, and not the classical or formal Greek of scholars and the upper class. The men God chose to write his word chose the language of the masses and communicated in ways that the masses could understand. The word was made accessible to the generality of people who in turn understood the message God intended the authors to communicate. Therefore, what the persons to whom they were addressed, i.e., the original audience/s, understood the text or entire books to mean is crucial to our own understanding of what the text or book means today.

Once more, textual interpretation must firstly proceed from, and adequate effort put in, discovering what the text meant in and of itself before seeking to know what it might mean for the reader today. We should not seek to approach the

Bible with a what-it-means-to-me posture. It does not and should not directly mean anything *to me.* The proper posture is *what it means in and of itself.* The Bible or a text thereof must mean something *in and of itself* before it means anything to me. We are reminded again that biblical truth is public, not private one (Article #3). We shall not read or seek to teach the Bible as if it is otherwise. It is possible for God's word to speak occasionally to us even out of context, but we should never normalize or make a habit of improper way of reading and understanding God's word. Nor should we seek to teach personal or private insights as doctrine or public truth, until it can be subjected to and affirmed by proper exegesis and community-hermeneutics of the body of Christ. Biblical truth, which must be received and preached or taught, is not derived from, or subject to our private, novel, or fanciful interpretations. The Bible means anything to the reader today only because it meant something to those who first received it. We must first discover what it meant to them before it can mean anything to us. It is what it meant to them that guides us into what the text means and how it applies to us today.

Article 10: Context Is Key

The Tenth Article of Biblical Understanding states that: Context Is Key - text without context is pretext

> *If my people who are called by my name humble themselves, and pray and seek my face and turn from their wicked ways, then I will hear from heaven and will forgive their sin and heal their land. 2 Chronicles 7:14*
>
> *First of all, then, I urge that supplications, prayers, intercessions, and thanksgivings be made for all people, for kings and all who are in high positions. 1 Timothy 2:1-2a.*

It is common practice to quote and apply (chapters and verses of) the Scriptures out of context. So commonplace a practice, in fact, that it hardly ever registers for many a believer as anomalous. That notwithstanding, we see that an interpretive effort of a stand-alone or orphan verse or text devoid of its context is pretentious exercise in misinterpretation. Context is everything in interpretating and understanding of text, and attempting any degree of interpretation out of context will lead inescapably to misinterpretation. A text, a book, or even a testament or the entire Bible itself is located and situated within layers of overlapping contexts. Context informs, guides and rules over interpretation of texts. No text or book or the Bible exists in isolation of other factors and influences altogether impacting it and being impacted by it.

So, what do we mean by *context* of Scripture? By context of a text of Scripture we mean the linguistic apparatuses, cognate texts and books, persons and peoples, events and places, and the socio-political, and religious-cultural influences which impact upon and help to properly locate and situate, elaborate, elucidate, enlighten, and enliven a text, book, or testament of Scripture. For our purposes we may group the context of text into five categories as *textual-linguistic, persons-peoples, historical- geographic/spatial, socio-political,* and *religious-cultural.* A particular text of Scripture may be impacted to a higher or lesser degree by all these five contexts.

We shall situate and review the two Scriptures quoted above—one each from Old and New Testaments—within their contexts. These passages appear to be often quoted out of context and interpreted by well-meaning Bible believers to either obligate God to hear and heal their different countries of Australia, Canada, Kenya, Nigeria, or USA (2 Chronicles

7:14); or to teach the Christian duty to pray for their leaders or worse still to teach praying for their leaders and governments as the citizen Christians' primary political duty in a polity *(1 Timothy 2:1-2a)*. Our review should alert us to the danger of quoting Scriptures out of context and further expatiate on how contexts help our proper interpretation and understanding of biblical texts.

Textual-linguistic context – by which we mean a group of held-together verses (i.e., paragraph/s or pericope) that expresses a central proposition, theme, or idea; issues of genre, grammar, and syntax. The biblical author used known words to construct sentences and paragraphs, according to known rules of grammar. Understanding those words and the rules of grammar and syntax leads to unlocking the meaning of texts. Note that a biblical text or pericope is not a verse of Scripture, but a group of verses which holds together to form and convey an idea, a proposition, a theme, or unit of thought. For example, the texts of our Scriptures above are 2 Chronicles 7:11-16 (extended, 2 Chronicles 6:12, 21-42, 7:11-16) and 1 Timothy 2:1-7 (extended 1 Timothy 1:18-2:1ff). Many English Bibles tend to identify (and sometime indent) pericopes for readers' convenience. Understand though that like the chapter and verse divisions, pericopes are not part of divine inspiration. For fuller contextual purposes, a reader or preacher may (and in many cases necessarily reference or) include verses or passages of Scripture in a pericope when it serves better sermonic, pedagogic or enrichment ends.

Persons-peoples context - by which we mean individual persons (including characters) or external others; specific or particular groups of people and/or ethno-linguistic people groups. In the OT text, this would include Solomon, the 2nd in what was going to be the Davidic dynasty, the First Temple Israelites ("my people"), the post exilic returnees including Ezra, Nehemiah and indirectly, Cyrus (Chronicles is believed to have been written (probably by Ezra) to encourage both the returnee and Judean Israelites and to set the agenda for a new people of God). The NT text will include Paul, Timothy, the Roman Emperor, emperor-cult religious leaders, governmental and city officials, and Ephesian non-believing peoples.

Historical-geographic/spatial context - by which we mean events, annals, chronicles, and narratives; geographic places, landmarks, and distances. In the OT text this is mostly historical events and accounts, Jerusalem and the first temple. In the NT text it would be the Greek city state of Ephesus.

Socio-political context – by which we mean social and political conditions and factors, local and distant kingdoms, rulers and rulership, economic affairs. In the OT text this should include the precedent and immediate social and political circumstances of the people of Israel—the Israel that was vis a vis the Israel that now is, to which the exiles returned. The NT text will include citizens and non-citizen statuses and minority-majority conditions and circumstances.

Religious-cultural context – by which we mean especially surrounding religions and religious thoughts and practices; cultures and cultural issues, concepts, and practices. The OT text will include Second Temple Judaic beginnings vis a vis First Temple Judaism, and to a lesser degree diaspora-returnee vs Judean (home-based) Jewish concerns. All these against the backdrop of Babylonish religious and cultural influences. The NT text will center around the beginnings of Paul's little flock, amid Jewish religious influences and Roman emperor cult.

With these contexts in view, we now turn to discovering what the meaning of our texts under review would be. So, we ask our first steps questions, situating the texts in their contextual locus: how would these contexts give us insight into the meaning of the texts? What did they mean to the original characters, audience, and author, in context? First the OT passage, *2 Chronicles 7:14.* We begin by situating the passage within the textual context of its pericope, i.e., 2 Chronicles 7:11-16, while keeping an eye on its larger textual context, i.e., 2 Chronicles 6:12, 21-42, 7:11-16. This helps us to get to the flow and main theme or central proposition of the text. We pay attention to word meanings, tenses, and sentence constructions. (For the average Bible reader, some helpful Bible study tools—parallel Bible translations, dictionaries and word studies, encyclopedias, and commentaries—may come in handy).

Looking at the text from the original audience-author perspective, we note that this was an address to post exilic Jews in the 5th century BC. The events chronicled by the author and involving the original characters of the narrative had occurred in the 10th century BC—some five hundred years earlier. The First (Solomon's) temple—the majestic symbol of God's presence among His people, and emblem of the divine approval of David and the Davidic dynasty—stood for over four hundred years until it was destroyed by the Babylonians in 587BC. Not only was the temple destroyed, but Jerusalem—the once *"great among the nations…princess among the provinces"*—was also decimated to the point of the elegy that is the book of Lamentations (cf. Lamentations 1:1ff.). This was the postexilic Israel that then was, all but totally abandoned for seventy years! Even the proposed new temple seemed, by comparison, to forlorn *"priests and Levites and heads of fathers houses, old men who had seen the first house,"* a pitiable replica, eliciting only deep sorrow and sadness (Ezra 3:12). It was the Israel—precarious, unstable, and a depressing shadow of its former glorious self—to which these diaspora Jews have now returned to confront. It was to them that the writer of Chronicles wrote.

How else would this prophet-chronicler begin to speak *"edification, encouragement and comfort"* to a dejected, deflated, and dithering people than a firm reaffirmation of God's covenant keeping faithfulness and their special place as God's covenant "my people." So, the chronicler wrote reminding them of the towering greatness of the Davidic-Solomonic era. He recalls in some details, especially, the greatness and prominence of Solomon's reign. He recounted Judah's (their forebearers) fall into sin, with echoes of Deuteronomic blessings and curses, the ultimate consequence of which was exile and captivity. The chronicler also noted Judah's godly kings, e.g., Hezekiah and Josaih. Their fall into sin notwithstanding, he also offered them hope, recalling God's faithfulness to his covenant people, his promise to forgive their sins—of which the return from exile is itself prime evidence—and restoration and reestablishment of the land of Israel.

It is in this context that we would begin to understand the Chronicler's purpose in narrating in elaborate detail the dedication of the great temple and Solomon's prayers. Crucial to the chronicler's objective of encouraging and motivating God's people was recalling Solomon's specific prayer requests, and God's specific promise of, forgiveness and restoration of God's covenant people. Note that the promise recounted in this text was strictly speaking made, not to the original audience, but to Solomon. The original author's intent was not for them to 'claim' this promise five hundred years later, but to demonstrate that God had indeed kept his promise to Solomon, and to encourage their confidence in God's sin-forgiving lovingkindness and promise-keeping faithfulness. Furthermore, it is to inspire hope for the potentiality of Israel's full restoration and future greatness even in the face of apparent hopelessness.

In writing the text, the author's three-part message to these Israelites were: a) your present circumstances and trauma of devastation, exile, return notwithstanding, you have a great heritage of great kings and kingdoms, b) Judah's fall into sin was the main cause of God's displeasure, take it seriously, but also note that your failure was not fatal, and c) God is a covenant-keeping faithful God; see what he promised our fathers and how he has kept them, and trust him going forward. We have arrived at this message by taking the context of the text seriously. It is the message of this this text, not the direct promise, which would be applicable to all peoples at all places. We would have more to say about application (cf. Article #12). The promise of the text was made specifically to King Solomon in reference to the actual natural covenant "my people" of Israel. The Holy Spirit caused this promise and its fulfillment among "my people" to be recorded to teach God's faithful promise-keeping nature to later generations. It was not intended simply as a promise to be claimed, and not by any other country, nation, or people—natural or spiritual.

Our New Testament text—*1 Timothy 2:1-2a.*—provides us a slightly different contextual perspective. Here, the original characters, author, and audience largely share the same contextual universe. Once again, we begin by situating the passage within the textual context of its pericope, 1 Timothy 2:1-7, with an eye on its larger textual context, 1 Timothy 1:18-2:1ff. The genre is epistolary (epistle or letter), and this text forms part of Apostle Paul's *"charge"* to his *"true child in the faith"* (Timothy) which began in chapter 1:18. Timothy was Paul's protégé, whom he had left in charge of the rudimentary missionary ministry in Ephesus while he (Paul) travelled to Macedonia via Troas (cf.1 Timothy 1:2, Acts 16:1f; 2 Timothy 4:13, Acts 20:1f). The Ephesus of Paul's day (of which we will have more to say in Article #12) was a Roman port city of Ephesus, which served as seat of the regional Roman governor. By ancient standards, Ephesus was a diverse city with a significant mix of Jews and gentiles, and religious freedoms.

An overview of Paul's missionary and epistolatory writings, clearly indicate an overarching teleological impetus driving his life and ministry. Paul was a pragmatic apostle with single-minded zeal and passion to know Christ and to make him known (cf. Acts 26:19; 1 Corith. 2:2; Phil. 1:21, 3:10). Paul's motto might as well have been: 'the whole gospel to the whole peoples by any means necessary.' In the specific text under review, we shall begin by noting that praying *"for all people, for kings and all who are in high positions* "or even "prayer" per se was not an end, for Paul, and sure not the goal of the text. The goal of, or the end to which the text drives, is *"that we may lead a peaceful and quiet life, godly and dignified in every way."* (v. 2b), or what we might like to refer to as the *moral society*. The outworking of the moral society—or the manifest kingdom *"your kingdom come"* (Matt. 6:10), in which our earthly communities begin to manifest the ideals of heaven—is the ultimate point of Paul's missiological enterprise. While and as the kingdom unfolds to its full manifestation, Paul in the meantime, had a more urgent goal, which was the advancement of the gospel and fulfillment of his missionary calling (vv.4-7). Achieving that urgent goal would only be possible for him and his acolytes if they could secure harmony with the civil authorities and within a peaceful, quiet, godly, and dignified first century Ephesian society.

For this band of Ephesian followers, Paul recommended prayer for civic leaders as a means towards achieving both the ultimate and proximate advantages of a well-ordered moral society. It is indeed not just religious cliche or Christianese—even if it might occasionally appear to be so for some—to say that "prayer is the master key." After all prayer at its core is attitude or disposition of utter dependence on God. To that end, prayer both motivates and undergirds all meaningful and enduring enterprises, including the emergence of the moral society. That said, it should be obvious that there were other—potentially more effective—means of achieving a well-ordered society than just prayers. The options would be many, such as active participation in the political processes of leadership selections, engagement with policy proposals and implementations, or even vying for and assuming civic leadership positions themselves.

It is highly improbable that Paul would recommend that all that Christians must do to achieve a moral society is just to pray—not even in Ephesus of today. Yet, Paul recommended prayers for these

Ephesian Christians of Timothy. Why? We will pick up on Ephesus at the time of Paul as contextual framework in a fuller discussion of the questions in Article #12. We will reckon with the socio-political, religious-cultural contexts of first century Ephesus which would have made it unlikely for Paul's band of followers to offer anything other than prayers. We would also see how improbable it would have been for Paul to enjoin just prayers for the realization of an ordered moral society for them, or for Christians in modern democracies today. Context will always remain indispensable to the interpretive framework for discovering the meaning of texts.

Article 11: If The Ordinary Meaning Of The Text Makes Sense, Do Not Seek Another Meaning

The Eleventh Article of Biblical Understanding state that: If The Ordinary Meaning Of The Text Makes Sense, Do Not Seek Another Meaning – make no room for fanciful, obscure, and peculiar interpretations.

> *But the natural man receiveth not the things of the Spirit of God: for they are foolishness unto him: neither can he know them, because they are spiritually discerned. 1 Corinthians 2:14 (KJV)*

The history of interpretations (and religion, itself) is replete with the tantalizing allure of "deep," "esoteric," and "hidden" meanings. From various forms of the mystic, esoteric, and gnostic, to animism, kabbalism, sufism and ever-mushrooming iterations of spiritualities. Man has always wondered at what lies beyond, and sought for knowledge beyond the realm and reach of mere mortals. "Masters," "guides," "gurus," "teachers," and "wise ones," have always arisen to lead the uninitiated into the inner sanctums of hidden gnosis, mysteries, and secret "truths." The allure of the obscure, the novel, the fanciful and allegorical "types and shadows" is so overwhelming for our inquisitive imagination to abjure.

Originally and before the Fall, God made humankind in His own image; and since the Fall, they say, humankind has sought to return the favor and remake God in humankind's image. In the image of God, we inherited our innate curiosity and capacity to imagine, explore, and discover. In the disfigurement of the fall, that fundamental trust in God's goodness and overflowing loving kindness morphed into distrust, suspicion, and too-good-to-be-true mode of relating. Our propensity to lie, and distrust in oneself and others, is projected on the divine. The simple must be complicated for it to have value and be meaningful. In a sin-laden dog-bite-dog existence, nothing good can be free—not even God can be trusted to freely give! Because we cannot take our own words at face value, God's word must as well not really be what God obviously means it to be. There must be something hidden behind the plain teaching of the word of God, we conclude.

Compounding the trust deficit crisis among Bible-believing readers sometimes, is an underlying anti-intellectualist fervor. For reasons embedded deep in the origins and history of faith, reason, rational thought, critical thinking, and overall intellectual enterprise tend to be mistrusted, antagonized, or barely tolerated in the church. How often, for instance, do we hear well-meaning people speak dismissively or derisively about seminary or divinity school training? How often do we hear otherwise rational persons make disparaging statements about academics, the academy, academic accomplishments, or the academic enterprise as if they are something less than? How often do we hear well-intentioned preachers make (pardon the choice of word) such most ignorant statements as "what I am giving you is not theology, what I am giving you is life," or suchlike, as if it is possible to make any statement whatsoever about God that is not *theology*?

Yes, it is also true that many a Bible-believer, including many a woman or man of God, may oftentimes seek to cover up or compensate for own inadequacies by projecting an aura of super spirituality as one having a secret conduit into the mind of the Spirit. Hence, men of God work hard to outdo themselves and each order in "discovering" and "prophetically" adducing "deeper," and far-fetched "spiritual" misinterpretations of clear and simple teachings of the Bible. To the extent the man of God inhabits and pontificates from this pedestal of gnosis, the unearned and pseudo-infallibility of the man of God is preserved, the thinking goes.

Recently, I stumbled upon a video clip of a well-known Nigerian apostle, in which the man of God employed the above-referenced (1 Corinthians 2:14 KJV) Scripture in self-assured dismissiveness of views contrary to his own on a topical theological issue. Aside from the cavalier out-of-context abuse of God's word—employing scriptural verses as pebbles to throw, or as cudgel to beat others into shape—there is a certain gnostic shtick embedded in employing scriptural verses in this manner. Of course, there is a spiritual dimension to full appreciation of scriptural truth, but that in no way absolves us from accountable and rational explication and explanation of what we believe and why we believe it. Good Christians can humbly come to different conclusions on theological or even textual matters without diminishing one another, provided they have utilized proper methods of biblical interpretation. Often, it is nothing short of prideful cover for our ignorance that make us run for cover under misuse of verses such as this. Moreover, we have already learnt enough to know that Paul was not teaching, in this Scripture, what our dear man of God thought Paul was saying here.

Paul's Corinthian audience were *"sanctified in Christ Jesus, called to be saints together with all those who in every place call upon the name of our Lord Jesus Christ, both their Lord and ours* (1 Corith. 1:2), and were *"not lacking in any gift"* (v.7). However, there had arisen among them some ungodly party-spirited *"divisions"* and *"quarreling,"* which could not be said to flow from, or represent the mind or spirit of Christ. Paul was so disgusted with the divisive jealousy and strife among them that although they were *"brothers,"* he (somewhat tongue in cheek) *"could not address [them] as spiritual people, but as people of the flesh, as infants in Christ* (3:1). This party spirit which Paul analogized rhetorically and equated with Greek philosophy which was this-worldly (soulish) was antithetical to the Jewish wisdom which was other-worldly (spiritual), just as one was temporal and the other eternal. In Paul's generalizing analogy, the "natural" person—such as the Greeks, who were solely dependent on intellect—could not evaluate the things of the (Judeo-Christian spirituality, or) *"Spirit."* Conversely, the *"spiritual"* person—such as the Corinthian *"saints,"* who, on the other hand, were guided and directed by the word of God (property interpreted, taught, and received) could evaluate all things—both Greek philosophical thought and Judeo-Christian religiosity.

Christians may have honest debates—and even disagreements (!)—about proper exegesis and hermeneutical decisions, or fine points of theological proposals and Christian practices. This in no way makes them *"natural men"* incapable of receiving *"spiritually discerned"* things. To the contrary, the refusal to properly interpret texts, and humbly submit one's decisions and tentative conclusions to the scrutiny of fellow mature believers because one has some secret insight into the private recesses of the mind of the Spirit is an ironic example of the natural man of which Paul was speaking. There is often, in some Bible believing Christians, an unwholesome dichotomization between the sacred and the secular, including bifurcating of the facility for accessing rational and spiritual knowledge.

However, such dichotomization is demonstrably unwarranted by Scripture or Pauline apostolic examples.

We can all say this together: *God is not daring humankind to a catch-me-if-you-can duel*! The scriptural witness is that God desires to be known; and He has made Himself known in the simplest and clearest ways possible. This might seem counter intuitive, after all his ways are as far from ours as the heavens are from the earth (cf. Isaiah 55:8f.). Not so fast, because Isaiah 55 is a poetic characterization of the magnanimity of God's compassion. It might sound contradictory, after all we had discussed the complexity of the word of God in Article #4. Not so, because it is not of God, but other contextual factors of peoples, times and places that complicate the simplicity of divine revelation. Imagine for a second that God choses to make Himself even slightly obscure, what chance do we puny, finite, mortals have to even begin to decipher the Holy One who *dwells in unapproachable light*?! In what theologians refer to as general revelation (cf. Psalm 19:1f.) the Psalmist points to all observable creation as ever-present display and reminder of the majesty, power and worth of God. God's self-disclosure in nature, though limited, is yet so revealing of God that only a fool could deny Divine Reality (cf. Psalm 13:1).

Many Bible-believing people tend towards tunnel-vision focus on the Bible (or a form of aristocratic biblicism) that they tend to lose the broader contextual forest in the Biblicist trees. Being too close, we tend to have a disjointed view of both Christianity and/or Judaism. If only as Joshua had admonished his people, we step back and get a thousand feet perspective of faith and Scriptures. If we did and get a better reframing view of our faiths and Scriptures, we would recognize that our faiths are ones of the underdog or the underclass. Christianity did not originate from the imperial palaces of Rome or even the high priestly courts of Second temple Judaism. Christianity originated in the margins—at the street corners of the underclass. No temples, no priests, nothing but the simplicity of an itinerant rabbi and a band of artisans and local fishermen. Its message was uncomplicated, its texts rudimentary and its language street. God made himself available to simple people in simple ways, communicating in simple language and in simple terms.

The Old Testament book of *Daniel* and New Testament book of *Revelations* may rank among the most difficult Bible books to read and interpret. What with the visions of battering rams and bodiless writing hands, hydra headed monsters, flying horses and sword wielding angels swarming the books. But, while some of the minute details, and the cryptic and apocalyptic language of the text may seem difficult for us to interpret today, the overall messages of the books are remarkably simple and easy to understand. Here again, the basic questions of authorial intent, the original audience's understanding and the contexts of the characters and actors come in handily to help us make sense of what might be going on in these books.

Both books were written by captive people to captive or somewhat captive peoples, and have similar messages. That being the case, the use of coded language, which was commonly and perfectly understood by both authors and audiences make perfect sense. To be clear, there was nothing particularly significant about the language and symbolisms of the books, except the convenience of using in-house lingo that the other side would not easily understand, and which would get us into trouble if they did. Think of how young Gazan men may communicate with each other under the watchful eyes and earshot of IDF soldiers. Or something as innocuous (?) as the gamut of emojis and SMS vocabulary young people read and write with dexterous fluency but which intended or not, leave parents and "ol' folks" totally baffled. Our difficulty today with say *Daniel* and *Revelation* is not with deciphering their overarching messages, but with interpreting some of the symbols used simply because of the distance between us and them, and the fact that we do not have access to their commonly understood coded lingo. So, what are the overarching messages of Daniel and Revelation? What would we learn from the contexts, original authors, and audiences?

Teenage Daniel was taken—together with some other youths and opinion leaders of Judah—into Babylon in ca 605BC under the reign of Babylonian King Nebuchadnezzar (2 Kings 23:34-24:6; Daniel

1:1-4). A second wave of deportations occurred in 597BC, which included taking more Jewish leaders, e.g. the prophet Ezekiel (2 Kings 24:6-16). Eleven years later in 586BC, the siege culminated in the destruction of both the temple and sacking of Jerusalem and the final deportation and beginning of the 70 years of Babylonian captivity (2 Kings 24:17-25:21). So, a covenant people who had hitherto followed and served a God they knew to be the Almighty, Sovereign Creator and Governor of the whole universe. A God who had made promises to their ancestors and kept those promises, from establishing them in the promised land, to the flowering of one of the most glorious reigns in the ancient world. A God who dwelt with them in a house built atop the city fortified and surrounded by the mountain of God's protection.

This same covenant people were now captives under the wicked kingdom of a ruthless and pompous uncircumcised pagan. Days turned into weeks, then months, and years. Soon anger gave way to disgust and sadness, to questioning and doubts. What became of his promises? Have our failures become fatal? Has God lost?

It was to those Babylonian captive Israelites that Daniel wrote a simple message of encouragement and hope: *amid the turmoil and turbulence of changing kingdoms and fortunes, the God of heaven will establish his kingdom on earth.* The kingdom God will establish shall overwhelm and supersede all earthly kingdoms, and sin and evil shall be eradicated from among men, forever. As weak, decimated and devastated as our Israel might be, and as powerful and strong Babylonian, Egyptian, Assyrian, and surrounding kingdoms might appear, no earthly king or earthly kingdom shall have the final say. God—our God, and the God of our ancestors—will have the final say. That was the message Daniel intended to pass on to his captivity audience. John the Revelator (of whom we will have more to say) was delivering an identical message to the suffering, desponded, and persecuted, and dying breed of believers in Asia minor. Amid all the twists and turns of human history, in the end, God wins and his people would be on the winning side.

Yes, exegeting texts will present varying degrees of difficulties and complexities. It will require a great deal of skill and practice to do it successfully. However, it is important to recognize that the overall messages of the books of the Bible and the Bible itself is quite simple. In Article #12 following we will further explore this need for approaching the Bible with the broad panoramic forest view before working through the nitty gritty of exegesis and textual interpretations. Understand that God wants to be understood, chose largely simple men and women to communicate his word in simple terms that all may know him. Ultimately proper exegesis and hermeneutics will require more sophistication and dexterity than is available to the average reader. For many of the reasons we have discussed under many of our rules, some biblical texts may present degrees of complexities that may be difficult to resolve or even reach a consensus. However, if the plain meaning of the text makes sense, do not look for another "deeper," "secret," or "spiritual" meaning. The author – divine-human – said what he meant and means what he said.

Article 12: Keep The Main Thing The Main Thing

The Twelfth Article of Biblical Understanding states: Keep The Main Thing The Main Thing – focus on the big picture—the grand narrative

> *"As soon as you see the ark of the covenant of the LORD your God being carried by the Levitical priests, then you shall set out from your place and follow it. Yet there shall be a distance between you and it, about 2,000 cubits in length. Do not come near it, in order that you may know the way you shall go, for you have not passed this way before." (Joshua 3:3)*

There is a sweet vantage spot which provides an observer with the best visual perception of that which is observed; and too close or too far away, acuity is distorted and perception unscrambled. Joshua had just taken charge and was leading Israel across Jordan into the promised land (cf. Joshua 3:1f). The formation put the ark of covenant-bearing Levitical priests in the lead, with the people matching out in tow behind the priests. The people, Joshua specifically instructed, must maintain a distance of 2000 cubits (a little above one-half mile) between them and the priests bearing the ark. They were strictly warned not to break formation and come any closer than this distance. Why—to what end? *"...in order that you may know the way you shall go, for you have not passed this way before"* (v.4). This we shall like to call the law of peripheral perception. It is not to lose the forest of universals for the trees of particulars.

The idea of peripheral perception is particularly important for biblical understanding. Typically, biblical hermeneutics or exegesis more so tend to focus on word studies, verb conjugations, sentence structures, diagraming and parsing, and the like.

Important as exegesis might be, it seems an inadequate starting point of biblical understanding. At the risk of belaboring the forest and tree analogy, when it comes to biblical interpretation and understanding the appropriate starting posture is to not lose the forest for the trees. That is not to wade into the minutiae of exegetical trees without a 2000-cubit peripheral perception of the entire scriptural forest. It is occupying that vantage spot and peering through the perceptual lens which reveals, informs, and clarifies what we see in texts, books and in the entire Bible.

In recap, we restate that hermeneutics involves the two main activities of discovering the meaning and message a biblical text; and passing that meaning and message to a contemporary audience. In other words, it is asking of a biblical text:

A. What does it mean?

B. What does it mean for us?

The task of discovering meaning is essentially a question of interpretation; while exploring what it means to us is a question of application. As we have discussed thus far, the subordinate questions implicated in discovering textual meaning includes:

1. What does it mean to original characters
2. What did it mean to the original author
3. What did it mean to the original audience? and
4. What did it mean in context?

To these four subordinate questions we shall now add a couple more that bring the text full circle and situate it properly in the holistic context of the entire Bible:

5. What does it mean in the light of the New Testament or Old Testament (depending if we are working vice versa with Old Testament of New Testament texts)? and
6. What does it mean in the light of the whole Bible?

These two (questions 5 and 6) analyze and relate the text—cross referencing word meanings, sentence structures, writing styles, etc.—with the other texts, the book and/or Testaments within which they are found, and the entire Bible. Each of the Old and New Testaments is complete and incomplete in of itself. There is clear anticipatory flair of the Old Testament, and a culminating distinctiveness about the New. Looking at the text from the perspective of the entire Bible (or what is sometimes loosely referred to as the tenor of the Bible) opens us to the overarching context of biblical interpretation. That is (hopefully) what is intended by the concept of letting Scripture interpret itself. Altogether, these six questions (as may or may not be relevant depending on the text under review), asked and properly answered lead us to the meaning and message of the text. However, the hermeneutic task is still incomplete.

The second and corresponding stage of the hermeneutical task lies with transferring and applying the meaning and message of the text to contemporary readers, i.e., readers today. Thus, the final hermeneutical question we bring to the text asks what it means for the readers today. Hence, the full plate of our hermeneutical questions are as follows: (see also Figure 6 Interpreting and Applying the Bible):

1. What does the text mean to original characters
2. What did the text mean to the original author
3. What did the text mean to the original audience? and
4. What did the text mean in context?
5. What does the text mean in the light of the New Testament or Old Testament (depending if we are working vice versa with Old Testament or New Testament texts)? and

6. What does the text mean in the light of the whole Bible?
7. What does the meaning or message of the text mean for us readers today?

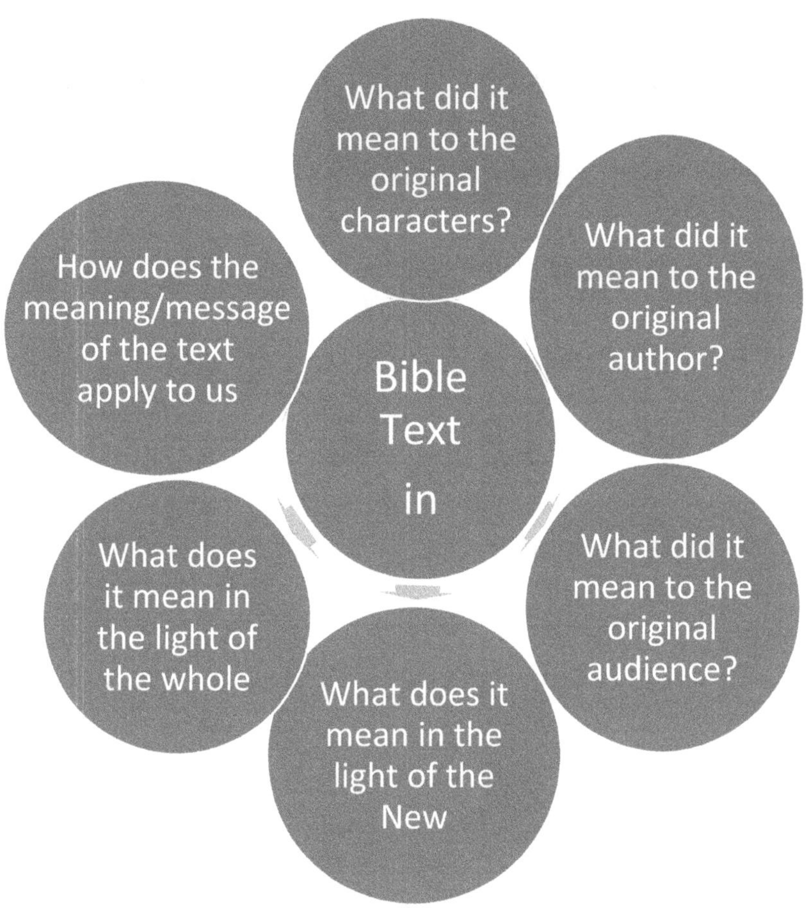

Figure 7 Interpreting & Applying the Bible—interrogating the text.

A couple more points of note. In practice, the biblical interpreter may find that the tasks of interpretation and application while distinct, do overlap and intersect as in the form of a "spiral."[24]

[24] Grant R. Osborne. *The Hermeneutical Spiral*, 1991 p6

We also reiterate that some biblical propositions, promises, commands, etc. may have direct universal applications. That said, it is crucially important to note that it is the meaning or message of the text, and not the direct language rendering—promise, commands, etc.—that apply word for word to today's reader.

There is yet a broader contextual framework within which the Bible itself is situated. The Bible—in both Testaments—grew out of confessional-worshipping communities of biblical Israelites and apostolic Christians. It is easy to forget, and misread our faith, by reading our contemporary realities back into its historical roots. Because we now have the complete canon of the Bible, we may sometimes be led to believe that the Christian faith simply grew out of the Bible, rather than the other round. We often fail to keep in mind that the stories of early Christianity, in its various forms were passed around within and across peoples and places as oral tradition, for close to fifty years before they were first put down in writing. Yes, the Bible is the word of God, but it is the word of God given to and through the confessional-worshipping community of believers. Hence, the brother contextual framework—the thread that ties Scriptures together—is that community forming *belief* that created and binds the community.

The Christian community grew out of a Judaic ethno-cultural-religious milieu within a Greco-Roman socio-political context. A small band of mostly Jewish peasants had followed Jesus—a

Jewish rabbi—whom they believed to be their Promised Messiah (the anointed or the Christ). Divinely appointed events culminating in Jesus' crucifixion and resurrection from death, and subsequent outpouring and enduement of the Holy Spirit on a Pentecost celebration changed everything, and confirmed for them the Person and Work of the Son of God! These otherwise dispirited band of mostly backwater Galileans were suddenly transformed and launched smack dab into the confluence of peoples, politics, and religions in Jerusalem, and beyond.

Without organization or structure, a priestly class, or developed theology and particular set of doctrines, they went about telling the story of the risen Lord. As they went, they struggled to understand for themselves, and define for others, both the *Person* and the *Way* of the movement. In doing so, they must explicate (especially to their fellow Jews) two apparently contradictory propositions: 1) that this Jesus was indeed the Promised Messiah and bona fide Mediator of the Covenant; and still somehow, 2) disassociate this Jesus from, and superimpose Him over the *old order* as the Mediator of the New (and better) Covenant. In other words, the continuity between the old order and Jesus—how Jesus connects with and continues the Covenant; and its discontinuity—i.e., where the old order stops and is superseded by Jesus. In simple terms, the story of Jesus the Christ—His Person and Works—became the forming *belief* which formed and informed the confessing-worshipping community of believers.

The *Christian* message was the very life of the early church, and its proclamation was its driving mandate. The church was not so much a confessing-worshipping or worshipping-missionizing community, but a missionizing-worshipping community, in that order. The primary task of the church—its *raison d'etre,* as it were—was to proclaim the good news of the kingdom (or messianic rule) of God among all peoples of the earth. Paul, for instance, would decidedly know nothing among his Corinthian audience *"except Jesus Christ and him crucified"* Corinthians 2:2 (ESV). And to the last days of the apostles and (shall we add) always, *"the testimony of Jesus is the spirit of prophecy"* (Revelations 19:10). Thus, the story of Jesus and the mandate to tell it, become the organizing perspective from which we must view Scriptures.

Consequently, in asking *"what does the text mean in the light of New Testament?"* or *"in the light of the Bible?"* we are indeed asking *"what does it mean in the light of Christ and His missionizing mandate?"* It is against that backdrop that we shall pick up our discussion of the text of 1 Timothy 2:1-7 (Article #10). *"What does this text mean in the light of the Christ?"* and, *"what might it mean for us today?"* Earlier on we have noted Paul's proximate intent in the text regarding the quest for an ordered moral society. We have also noted Paul's urgent and grander purpose of the text as a well-ordered society being essential for Paul's all-consuming missional passion, (v. 5; cf. Philippians 3:7f.; 1

Corinthians 2:2). We also noted that while prayer is critically important in the lives of church and society, it was hardly a most effective way of effectuating an ordered society. So, it is crucial to the meaning of the text to interrogate Paul's reasoning in recommending prayers instead for the Ephesian believers.

As indicated, this has everything to do with the socio-political context of Ephesus of Paul and Timothy's time. Paul's pastoral letter was written ca 62-66AD. Paul had entrusted his protégé Timothy with the charge of his fledgling evangelistic ministry in this Roman port city, which also served as seat of the regional Roman governor. Its diverse subject peoples—especially monotheistic Jews—were exempted from pagan and emperor worship. They were allowed to pray and offer sacrifices *for* but not *to* the emperor. Paul and the Ephesian believers were already embattled at least from two fronts—from the legalistic Judaizers and subversives, the likes of Hymenaeus and Alexander (1 Timothy 1:3f.) on one hand, and antagonists and shriners, the likes of Demetrius (Acts 19:23ff.) on the other. They could ill afford opening of yet another front with the local civil authorities.

A well-ordered and decorous society is itself virtuous, but for Paul's additional end, it further guarantees the accessibility and flourishing of the gospel. Being most probably composed of subject peoples, the believers were enjoined to pray for the emperor and for *"all who are in high positions"* (1 Timothey 2:1). These people in high positions were likely appointed by the emperor or elected by citizen Ephesians. By praying for the emperor and the people he had appointed (or elected by the citizens) into high positions, these subject peoples (Ephesian believers) showed themselves as good members of the society in which they lived. Again, prayer is very important, but not the normal or most efficient means of appointing leadership and securing a well-ordered society. That being so, it would have been ludicrous of Paul to have recommended prayers for his group if they were composed exclusively or mostly of *Cives Romani* (full Roman citizens).

So, we learn from the text that the pursuit of a well-ordered and moral society is a virtuous and worthy endeavor. A well-ordered society is beneficial for public good as well as for the furtherance of the gospel. Christians especially minority or non-citizen Christians should seek and maintain the goodwill of host or majority civil authorities provided Christian principles are not compromised. Citizen Christians shall live up to their citizenship responsibilities and engage every means necessary, as dictated by the circumstances and structures of their own contexts, towards the actualization and sustenance of a well-ordered and moral society.

Again, prayer is a given in all Christian endeavors, but not surprisingly, prayer per se or prayers for those in positions of authority, is not the primary responsibility of citizen Christians in a polity, nor is it the goal of this text. In a modern democratic nation-state, for instance, God's primary method of appointing leadership and securing good governance for the people is through the political and policy processes. Therefore, citizen Christians in modern democratic nation-states such as Australia, Canada, Kenya, Nigeria, or USA may well pray. But they are enjoined to engage fully in the political and policy processes of their respective countries for the actualization of that *"peaceful and quiet life"* which is *"godly and dignified in every way,"* and that is *"good… and pleasing in the sight of God our Savior (1 Timothy 2:2, 3).*

What a text means in the light of Christ—especially an Old Testament text—involves accounting for the relationship between the Old Order and the New. We have already noted the original struggles of the apostles in properly situating the Jesus story within the continuity-discontinuity spectrum of the Old and New Covenants. These struggles we shall see highlighted in a pair of New Testament books: the *Epistle to the Galatians,* and the *Epistle to the Hebrews,* respectively. In *Galatians* the relationship between the New Covenant and the Mosaic law was explored in a general way, and in *Hebrews* the more pointed and significant question of the superiority of the messianic and priestly credentials of Jesus the Christ juxtaposed and contrasted with those afforded by the Old Covenant. In the same vein, the books will provide us with helpful ways of deducing authorial intent through internal and external evidentiary contexts of the book itself, even when it is not specifically indicated.

The Epistle to the Galatians - Who Has Bewitched You? Paul wrote the *Epistle to the Galatians*—his first and earliest book of the New Testament (save James) sometime between 48-55AD. The other epistles and gospels will follow subsequently. (Note that we read the New Testament backwards when we read from the Gospels to the Epistles). *Galatians* was addressed to groups of substantially non-Jewish churches, in the regions of Galatia (modern Turkey, (1:2)). Paul's purpose of writing was to counter those who taught that the followers of Christ must submit to the Judaic order and observe circumcision to be received by God. Paul became alarmed and was *"astonished"* that the Galatian believers were abandoning *"the grace of Christ"* and turning to a *"different gospel"* (Galatians. 1:6), which indeed was no gospel at all. The token of their abandonment of grace of Christ and turning to this *different gospel* was the Galatian recourse to Mosaic law with its commandments and ordinances, which Paul refers to as *"the weak and worthless elementary principles of the world"* (Galatians 4:9; cf. Romans 8:3; Hebrews 7:18).

In a way of speaking, we see Paul here already providing some answers to our final question about meaning: what does it mean in the light of New Testament/Christ? In Paul, Christ is the key that unlocks the meaning of Christian godliness. In similar fashion, this central message of Paul was captured for instance in Romans 10:4, *"Christ is the end of the law for righteousness to everyone who believes."* And, in *Ephesians,* God in Christ has abolished *"the law of commandments expressed in ordinances, that he might create in himself one new man in place of the two, so making peace"* (2:15). Here in *Galatians,* the specific emblem of the subversion of the gospel of grace was the demand by the Judaizers of adherence to the ordinance of circumcision upon gentile Galatians. For Paul, the enduring meaning and message embedded in the commands may apply to gentiles, but not the direct commands as if the gentiles were Jews to whom the commands were directly made.

Circumcision was in fact commanded by God, and was Abrahamic and pre-law. But the break with the old order was so fundamental and the stakes so high that Paul could only view this subversion of grace in demonic terms: *"O foolish Galatians! Who has bewitched you"* (3:1)? The Galatian believers were reminded that they were not at liberty to pick and choose when it comes to old order/Mosaic ordinances. For as Jacob would say: *"For whoever keeps the whole law but fails in one point has become accountable for all of it."* (James. 2:10). So, Paul continues to remind them, it is all or nothing: *"Cursed be everyone who does not abide by all things written in the Book of the Law, and do them."* (Galatians 3:10). And, speaking specifically about the circumcision ordinance: *"If you accept circumcision, Christ will be of no advantage to you"* (5:3). Why so? *"I testify again to every man who accepts circumcision that he is obligated to keep the whole law. You are severed from Christ, you who would be justified by the law; you have fallen away from grace."* (Galatians 3:3, 4). It was that serious, and as an aside, we could only imagine how mortified Paul would be, were he to appear and see the modern Christian fetishization of Judaic symbols and religious renaissance.

The Epistle to the Hebrews—Christ is Better. The Epistle to the Hebrews was written in the late 60s AD, ca. ten years later than Galatians. Though coming later in writing, the Judaic-Christian continuity-discontinuity tension (especially for our purposes) is better sketched out in *Hebrews* than in *Galatians*. The original author is unknown, although tradition often attributes it to Paul. The original audience to which *Hebrews* was written was (predominantly) Jewish community of believers struggling with how to square this Jesus with everything they had always known about God and Jewry—the torah, covenant, community, temple, commandments, and ordnances. Compared and were reminded that they were not at liberty to pick and choose when it comes to old order/Mosaic ordinances. For as Jacob would say: *"For whoever keeps the whole law but fails in one point has become accountable for all of it."* (James. 2:10). So, Paul continues to remind them, it is all or nothing: *"Cursed be everyone who does not abide by all things written in the Book of the Law, and do them."* (Galatians 3:10). And, speaking specifically about the circumcision ordinance: *"If you accept circumcision, Christ will be of no advantage to you"* (5:3). Why so? *"I testify again to every man who accepts circumcision that he is obligated to keep the whole law. You are severed from Christ, you who would be justified by the law; you have fallen away from grace."* (Galatians 3:3, 4). It was that serious, and as an aside, we could only imagine how mortified Paul would be, were he to appear and see the modern Christian fetishization of Judaic symbols and religious renaissance.

The Epistle to the Hebrews—Christ is Better. The Epistle to the Hebrews was written in the late 60s AD, ca. ten years later than Galatians. Though coming later in writing, the Judaic-Christian continuity-discontinuity tension (especially for our purposes) is better sketched out in *Hebrews* than in *Galatians*. The original author is unknown, although tradition often attributes it to Paul. The original audience to which *Hebrews* was written was (predominantly) Jewish community of believers struggling with how to square this Jesus with everything they had always known about God and Jewry—the torah, covenant, community, temple, commandments, and ordnances. Compared and contrasted with all these the original author was to make the bold and decisive point that Christ is better, greater, or superior.

The Christ of *Hebrews* is the eternal *"Son,"* and *"the radiance of the glory of God, "*(1:2, 3) whom as such is *"much superior to angels"* (v.4). Christ *"Jesus has been counted worthy of more glory than Moses"* (3:3), the *"guarantor of a better covenant"* (7:22); having obtained *"a ministry that is much more excellent that the old covenant"* 8:6). Infinitely more efficacious than *"the blood of goats and calves"* (9:11f.), the *"blood of Christ, who through the eternal Spirit offered himself without blemish to God, purify our conscience from dead works to serve the living God."* With full assurance of faith in the once-and-for-all, eternal-redemption-securing sacrifice (10:1f.), through which God *"had provided something better for us"* (11:40), and the *"mediator of a new covenant,"* the believers could rest with full confidence in a far superior advocacy before the Father (cf. 12:24). And living thusly with *"brotherly love,"* and offering *"such sacrifices…pleasing to God,"* they could one and all say with confidence: *"The Lord is my helper; I will not fear; what can man do to me?"* (13:1ff.).

About the knottier question of priesthood, in particular, the author would have to first wrestle with a fundamental dilemma. Jesus did not come from the tribe of Levi, but *"descended from Judah, and in connection with that tribe Moses said nothing about priests"* (Hebrews 7:14). That being the case, he could not possibly qualify for a valid priestly office, knowing that Aaronic priesthood is hereditary, and exclusively reserved for the tribe of Levi. If Jesus lacked the pedigree of legitimate priesthood, he could be nothing more than an impostor without any rights of vicarial functions. And if so lacking of the most basic qualification of priesthood, any claim of Christ's mediatory role—not to talk of possessing a superior priesthood—a nullity. This, as it were, was the theological Kilimanjaro the original author of *Hebrews* had to scale. Unlike in *Galatians* the issue here in *Hebrews* is by far a bigger theological fish to fry than figuring how to incorporate decadent Judaic ordnances into Christianity. At issue is the very essence of the Christian self-understanding and apostolic gospel. The entire Christ event, his vicarious death and atonement for the sin of mankind stands or collapses on this point. For as Paul would write to his Corinthian audience, *"if Christ has not been raised, your faith is futile and you are still in your sins"* (1 Corinthians 15:17).

In working out this theological conundrum, the original author reaches back and finds something analogous in the *"priesthood"*25 of Melchizedek (cf. Genesis 14; Psalms 110). Firstly, he argues the inherent weakness and temporariness of Aaronic priesthood—together with its commandments, ordinances, and sacrifices—demonstrating that *"perfection [was not] attainable through the Levitical priesthood"* (Hebrews 7:11f, cf. 8:13). Secondly, he argues for the superiority and eternality of Jesus' priestly office—who as *"the Son of God he continues a*

[25] Intertestamental scriptures did not describe Melchizedek as a priest, but as having priestly functions, cf. 11QMelch 2:6, DSS. This is also important in understanding the nature of Christ's and believers' "priesthood." Strictly speaking, neither Jesus—and by extension, non-tribal Levites—could be priests, even if they may possess priesthood and perform the priestly office.

priest forever" (Hebrews 7:3, 17, 20; 8:1ff. 10:8; cf. Psalms. 110:4). But, granting Jesus' priestly credentials, how would he compare—no less supersede—father Abraham?! This would have been such a theological tall order, for as John would later report in the Gospel that bears his name of *"the Jews"* querying Jesus, *"are you greater than our father Abraham, who died"* (John 8:53)? Moses mediated the torah and founded the Jewish faith, of which the Aaronic priesthood was an integral component (cf. Hebrews 3:3; 8:5f). But *Abraham* was on a different league. He was the founder of the Jewish people. To him God gave the (Abrahamic) covenant and the promises (Genesis 12; Hebrews 6:13f. 11:17).

Here the writer of Hebrews strove, as it were, to kill (or make alive) the proverbial two birds with one stone. He chose Abraham's giving of tithe to the enigmatic Melchizedek (Hebrews 7:1f. cf. Genesis 14). In the same manner of Jesus's non-genealogical ties with the tribe of priests, so was Melchizedek. With no genealogical record or succession, thus *"resembling the Son of God,"* Melchizedek lives in the collective memory as *"a priest forever"* (7:3, cf. Psalm. 110:4). *Forever young!* The Aaronic priesthood is based on genealogical succession. Melchizedek's was not.

Exclusive priesthood of the Levitical family and their receiving of tithes from their brethren Israelites emblematized privilege and degree of hierarchal superiority. Being the ancestral progenitor of the Jews, Abraham was obviously genealogically superior to Levi. So, having already argued that Abraham giving tithe to Melchizedek is indicative of Melchizedek's superiority over Abraham (7:7), he now stretches the tithe analogy almost to a breaking point. Levi—the ancestor of the Levitical family—was a long way from being conceived, yet *"one might even say that Levi himself paid tithes through Abraham"* (7:9). He argues, *ipso facto,* Melchizedekian priesthood has preeminence over Aaronic priesthood.

The *Hebrews* writer's argument, which fitted nicely with prevailing theological reflections of intertestamental Judaic environment, was simple: there is a preeminently superior, non-hereditary priestly "order" (relative to which the Aaronic one may be considered a shadow (cf. Heb. 9:11)); and, Christ's is of that "order" (5:5, 5; 7:17). More importantly, his audience were to understand that Christ Jesus was not only a suitable mediator but in fact the better Mediator of a superior Covenant (Hebrews 8:1; 9:11, 12, 15; 10:11, 12). *"For by a single offering he has perfected for all time those who are being sanctified"* (Heb. 10:14). The author's intention in invoking Melchizedek and Abraham was to argue for the superiority of Jesus' priestly office. The Incarnate Son as the Mediator of the New Covenant was and remains the profound concern of the Holy Spirit here as well as the entire book. Throughout their history and in a variety of ways, God mediated His name, His nature, and His glory to the Jewish people through the prophets, *"but in these last days he has spoken to us by his Son, whom he appointed the heir of all things, through whom also he created the world"* (Hebrews 1:2f.). The expected *"messenger of the covenant"* (Malachi 3:1), who is *"the image of the invisible God "*(Colossians 1:15), and *"the radiance of the glory of God"* (Hebrews 1:2), is he in whom *"the whole fullness of deity dwells bodily"* (Colossians 2:9).

In the Gospels, our Lord Jesus, the Christ Himself, explained to those two distraught and dejected brethren down on Emmaus Road how He the Christ was the hermeneutic lenses through which to view and understand the Tanakh (Hebrew Bible, (Luke 24:27)). And the illumination Christ brought on the text made their *"hearts burn within"* them while he *"opened the Scriptures"* (v. 30) to them. We read John's declared purpose of writing the gospel that bears his name, that his audience might *"believe that Jesus is the Christ, the Son of God, and that by believing you may have life in his name* (John 20:31). Paul lamented the blindness of his Judaic religious brothers in not recognizing Christ as the goal (telos) of the entire Torahic structure (cf. Romans 10:1f). It is the Christ, who alone is *"the Alpha and the Omega, the first and the last, the beginning and the end"* (Revelation 22:13), the conquering *"Lion of the tribe of Judah,"* the *"Root of David,"* that can *"open the scroll and its seven seals"* (Revelation 5:6). A Christocentric perspective gives us the best interpretative grid to study and understand—and to draw out and apply the meaning and message of—the Bible.

In affirming and understanding Christ as the fundamental interpretive grid through which all Scriptures is read and understood, two important caveats or notes are in order. Firstly, Christ is profoundly much more than His works. It is tragic diminishment of the Person and work of the Lord to see him merely as a miracle worker or a moral teacher. Jesus did and still does miracles, but Jesus is not just a miracle worker. In the texts of the New Testament, Christ's miracles were noted as signs and wonders. Wonders, are acts and events purposed to excite amazement, draw attention, and sustain curiosity and interest. Signs are symbolic in that they point to greater reality. An "evil and adulterous generation" will always *"seek for a sign"* (cf. Matthew 12:39). Jesus' miracles were not ends in of themselves, but pointers to who he was as the Son of God and expected Messiah. As C. S. Lewis will remind us in his *Mere Christianity*[26] Christ is not

---

[26] C. S. Lewis, *Mere Christianity*, 1952, pp. 55-56.

just a great moral teacher. He is the Son of God…Lord and God!

A second caveat about Christ as the Bibles' interpretive grid is being careful not to see Christ in all and every text, or force Him into texts where He is not. It is interpreting Scriptures from the vantage perspective of the revelation of Christ as the overarching explanation and purpose of Scriptures. It is not necessarily true that there is Christ in every book—no less every chapter—of the Bible. There are, of course, true typologies in the Bible. Both Paul and the writer of the book Hebrews, respectively, wrote about "*the written code*" (i.e., the Jewish ceremonial law (Colossians 2:14, NIV cf. Hebrews 10:1)) and the priestly order of the old covenant (cf. Hebrews 8:1f.) as "*shadow* [Gk. *skia,* i.e., prefigure] *of things to come*" (Colossians 2:17), or "*of the heavenly things*" (Hebrews 8:5). In same vein, both writers contrasted "*the present Jerusalem*" which was "*in slavery with her children*" (Galatians 4:25), with the "*heavenly Jerusalem*" (Hebrews 12:22), "*which is above*" and "*is free*" (Colossians 4:26). Great care must always be exercised in identifying, isolating, and clarifying true typologies in the Bible. There is no warrant to categorize or view entire texts, books, or the Old Testament, for example, in terms of so-called typologies. It is important to understand the typological genres where rhetorical devices adopted from the philosophies and languages of the time, and were employed to drive home the authors' points. There is no biblical warrant or interpretive value in divesting texts, characters, objects and/or events, of their actualities in the name of ‘types and shadows.’ Such flippant categorization of ‘types and shadows’ often lead to wild and fanciful distortions, misinterpretation of texts, and misunderstanding of the meaning and message of the Bible.

The Scriptures is the story of God and man in covenantal-redemptive relationship. The purpose of the Scriptures is to make us know God and in knowing, worship God better; or in the words of the Westminster Catechism, “to glorify God and to enjoy him forever.” Christ the Eternal Son of God who took flesh as the Messenger of the Covenant and Example of loving-obedience serves as the both the focal point and peripheral perception context through which we understand what it means to live in covenant relationship with God. To be properly guided through the *labyrinthian wilderness* that is the Bible, we need our gaze firmly focused on the divine North Star—the light that lightens and illuminates all of God's revelation. Thus, the Christ of the New Testament becomes the explainer that explains the entire revelation of God to humankind. Hence, the *Christian*—Missions-centric or Christo-centric—perspective of biblical interpretation is the overarching context or perspective that sheds light on and explains all of Scriptures. Keep the main thing the main thing!

Bibliography

Bruce, F. F., & J. I. Packer, Philip Comfort, Carl F. H. Henry. *The Origin of the Bible.* Laridian (http://www.laridian.com).

DeRouchie, Jason S. 2017. *How to Understand and Apply the Old Testament; twelve steps from exegesis to theology.* P & R Publishing

Naselli, Andrew David. 2017. *How to Understand and Apply the New Testament; twelve steps from exegesis to theology*. P & R Publishing.

Osborne, Grant R. 1991. *The Hermeneutical Spiral; a comprehensive introduction to the principles of biblical interpretation* (Expanded Edition). InterVersity Press.

Thiselton, Anthony C. 1997. *New Horizons in Hermeneutics: the theory and practice of transforming biblical reading* (20th Anniversary Edition) (Revised edition). Zondervan *Academic.*

Vanhoozer, Kevin J. 2009. *Is There a Meaning in This Text? The Bible, the Reader, and the Morality of Literary Knowledge* (10th Anniversary edition). Zondervan Academic

www.ingramcontent.com/pod-product-compliance
Lightning Source LLC
LaVergne TN
LVHW010542160826
845677LV00013B/2961

* 9 7 8 9 7 8 7 9 1 3 8 3 3 *